M000221619

Memoirs of a Papillon

Memoirs of a Papillon

Papillon

The Canine Guide to Living with
Humans without Going Mad

Genevieve
(as told to Dennis Fried, Ph.D.)

Eiffel Press

Manufactured in the United States of America
Library of Congress Control Number: 00-132251
ISBN: 0-9679335-0-1
Book design and production: Tabby House
Front cover photo: Pets by Paulette, Sarasota, Florida

Eiffel Press
431 Oak Point Road
Osprey, FL 34229
eiffelpress@verizon.net

This book is dedicated to
animal rescue workers everywhere.

Contents

Appendix

Preface

The origins of the papillon breed are uncertain. One theory holds that the breed traces its lineage back to the ancestors of the Mexican Chihuahua, brought to Europe by returning Spanish conquistadors in the sixteenth century. This theory, however, is undermined by the presence of very papillon-looking dogs in Italian paintings created as early as the fourteenth century. This has led many to conclude that the papillon is a descendant of the Italian toy spaniel, now extinct. In any case, the papillon evolved most noticeably in France and Belgium during the sixteenth and seventeenth centuries. Papillons were a popular companion to the nobles and aristocrats of that era, and legend has it that Marie Antoinette carried her pet papillon with her to the guillotine (presumably she relinquished it before keeping her appointment).

"Papillon" in French (pronounced "pah-pea-yon") means butterfly, and the name was bestowed on the breed because the erect ears are reminiscent of butterfly wings. A papillon whose ears droop like a spaniel's, an acceptable variation, is known as a phalene, from the French word meaning moth. Papillons are relatively uncommon in the United States. For example, American Kennel Club statistics reveal that the most popular purebred dog, the Labrador retriever, added 154,897 new registrations during the year 1999. In contrast, the papillon, forty-sixth on the list, had 3,547 new registrations during that period. Millions of people were introduced to the breed for the first time while watching "Kirby" win the prestigious Best in Show award at the televised 1999 Westminster Kennel Club Dog Show.

Papillons are invariably described as energetic, elegant, friendly, intelligent, affectionate, playful, alert, possessive, and strong-willed. Does Genevieve exhibit any of these traits? That will be left for you to decide as you read her story.

There will be skeptics who insist that I am the true author of this book, not Genevieve. Allow me to set the record straight at the outset. Genevieve wrote this book by her actions, attitude, expressions, and indomitable personality. Granted, I typed the words but the content is all Genevieve's.

In spite of the title, this is not a book about papillons. Rather, it is the celebration of a gift: the wondrous and loving relationship that exists between two denizens of an infinitely empty universe—dogs and people.

Finally, we would like to thank both Filou and Walt Rothenbach for their kind permission to reprint their letters in Chapter 15.

Enjoy.

DENNIS FRIED

Memoirs of a Papillon

The Canine Guide to Living with Humans without Going Mad

1

My First Two Months

I was born on December 19, 1997, in Venice, Florida, and I don't remember a thing about it. My earliest memories are of being kept warm and well fed by a big, furry milk-dispenser. I also remember getting banged around by two much smaller, smoother furbags. It took me two weeks to gather up the courage to open my eyes for the first time, and when I did I saw my mother, Chloe, my sister, Heidi, and my brother, Hunter. My name, I soon learned, was Hannah.

We three little ones were confined to a pen in the corner of a room. This arrangement suited me just fine because it gave me a feeling of power to know that I could pee all over my entire personal universe. Chloe could jump in and out of the pen whenever she wanted, and sometimes she'd leave and take a short vacation. I didn't like it when she was gone, but she always came back because she loved us.

Two other big girls would appear from time to time and jump into our pen with us—my half-sisters, Cecily and Emma. They were extremely interested in us babies, but they had a fit whenever we nibbled on their faucets to try to get a drink. Sometimes they played a little too rough with us, and Chloe would have to ask them to leave us alone. When they wouldn't listen, Chloe nipped them on the butt to underline her point. This seemed to work extremely well, and it served as an early lesson for me in the art of social persuasion.

Another creature lurked around the house, too. I would have guessed it to be a dog, but even at that young age I knew that no dog could be that ugly. It turned out to be a cat. It didn't seem to have an identifiable purpose in life, spending most of its time vegetating on tables and windowsills staring at things, including me. I found it amazing that a living thing could be so inert for so long without belonging in a flowerpot.

I learned from Chloe that my daddy was named Calvin, although several times she tried to explain to us that she had never really "been with" Calvin at all. Whatever it was she meant by this, I didn't know whether I was supposed to be mad or glad. I would have asked Calvin about it, but he never came around to see us. Chloe said he was too busy running around town being a stud for all the pretty ladies. She didn't specify whether this activity was of the "been with" or the "not been with" kind.

My first human friend was Sharon, who was there from the beginning helping Chloe take care of us all. She made sure that Chloe always had plenty to eat and drink, and she kept putting nice clean newspapers down in our pen for us to read. That was the beginning of my desire to be a writer when I grew up. She also brought us toys and played with us and cuddled us, giving poor Chloe quiet time to take much-needed naps.

When we were old enough to walk and run, Sharon would carry us all into the living room and let us play games with the big dogs. My favorite game of all was doggy football. The object was to grab the little football and try to run off the living room carpet with it for a score. The other dogs had to tackle you and force a fumble, then try to grab the ball and score themselves. We babies would sometimes get so excited that we'd have to go potty right in the middle of the playing field. Sharon watched us closely and, like a good coach, if she saw one of us start to hunch up she would take us out of the game.

I loved it at Sharon's Home for Unwed Mothers. When we were big enough to go outside by ourselves, we had the run of a big, beautiful yard with lots of trees and even a pond to splash around in. Chloe taught us to chase squirrels and lizards and to bark at birds that would laugh at us from the trees. Birds aggravated me; I couldn't understand how they could jump so high. I tried it by running fast and hopping, but something was wrong with my technique. I thought that maybe when I got older I would figure it out and then those birds would be in for a nasty surprise.

As the weeks passed, I became bigger and stronger and smarter. I tipped the scales at three whole pounds and was feeling that I could whip the world. (As long as Chloe was close by, that is.) Sharon had lots of human friends that came to visit us. Some of them had babies of their own. These baby humans were a lot older than I was, but some of them couldn't even walk yet! They just lay around and made gurgling noises from both ends. There was absolutely no chance of them playing doggy football with us. My early exposure to humans really got me wondering about them, and I decided to embark on an intensive study of these strange beings. If I was going to have to live with humans, it would be to my advantage if I could thoroughly understand how they operated. Since they seemed much less developed than dogs, I didn't anticipate any difficulties.

One afternoon Sharon had another visitor, a human named Katrina. She told Sharon that people called her Kat for short, but she was a lot prettier than any cat I'd ever seen. She sat down on the floor and played with all of us for a long time, but she seemed to be watching me especially closely. I finally got tired and tried to crawl under a chair to take a little dognap, but she pulled me out and made me play some more. She also was asking a lot of nosy questions about me. What was my personality like? (*Excellent.*) Did I eat well? (*Just ask poor Chloe.*) Did I seem to like people? (*In controlled doses.*) Was I for sale? (*Huh?*)

At last she left and that was fine with me. I could hardly have known then how much my life was about to change.

2

How Katrina Persuaded Denny to Get Me

Katrina's husband, Denny, has a friend back in his hometown of Catskill, New York, a venerable, black guru of life and, more specifically, women. Among the many basic principles taught by "Doc" are (1) never let a woman have the key to your apartment—because then the apartment isn't yours anymore, (2) never tell a woman "I love you"—because then she holds the power and will use it against you, and (3) never have fewer than seven girlfriends at any particular time because you shouldn't go out with the same woman more than once a week. Although Denny was unable to uphold any of these principles for most of his adult life, Doc continued to hold out hope for him. But Doc's most fundamental principle, and the foundation of all the others, is that "the dumbest woman is smarter than the smartest man." This Denny was able to accept without reservation, having failed to understand the thought process of any woman he had ever met. Still, Denny could not imagine any way that a woman, no matter how much smarter she might be, was ever going to persuade him to add a dog to his purposely very short list of life's responsibilities.

It wasn't that Denny didn't love dogs. When he was fourteen years old a beautiful, little white mutt with brown ears and a brown spot on his back appeared mysteriously on his street one summer afternoon. He was collarless and friendless and only a few months old. Denny and his younger brother, Randy, fed the hungry pup some milk and tied a rope loosely around his neck for a leash. They took the pup to the police station, but there was no report of a missing dog. The policeman said that if no one claimed the dog within two weeks, they could keep it or give it up to the pound, where it would be "put down" (that was the phrase the policeman used) if it was not adopted in a reasonable amount of time.

They rushed home, their new friend trotting happily beside them. A family summit meeting ensued and the parental powers laid down the law: Denny and Randy could keep the dog for two weeks, but if no one claimed him by then he had to go to the pound. You see, their mom and dad had owned a dog early in their marriage and loved it dearly. It was only a few years old when someone stole it from their backyard. They were so heartbroken that they vowed never to be vulnerable to such hurt again—no more pets! Ever.

With the two-week reprieve in hand, Denny and Randy spent the afternoon building a luxurious doghouse out of scrap building material donated by a neighbor. It had an overhanging shingle roof, tile interior, and wall-to-wall carpeting. It also weighed thousands of pounds and they needed their dad's help to move it to the shady part of their fenced-in yard.

Kids like to call each other names, especially nonsense names they've made up themselves. For reasons now lost to history, for many months Denny and Randy had been calling each other "dumb sardo" at every opportunity. As they built the doghouse, Denny would drop the hammer and be a "stupid sardo." Randy would bring the wrong board and be nothing but a "dumb sardo." The pup, of course, was now one of them, so when his barking became especially shrill as they completed his house it was natural enough to tell him to "Shut up, you dumb sardo." By the end of the afternoon, the pup had a name: Sardo.

They couldn't wait to see how Sardo looked in his new house, so they led him over and tried to coax him in. He wanted no part of it. They picked him up and put him in. He came running right out. They tried it again. He was out like a shot. All that work for nothing. They thought that maybe Sardo didn't like the carpet they'd picked out. For the next two days they tried everything to get him to stay in his house. They threw dog biscuits in. He'd duck in, grab the treat, and run right back out. They crawled into the house themselves and called him. He'd just look at them as if they were nothing but dumb sardos.

So the first two nights Sardo slept under the stars, just outside the backdoor, while his gleaming bachelor pad remained as vacant as a certain house in Amityville. On the third evening a hard rain began to fall. Denny and Randy ran to the window and looked out into the yard. And there, barely visible in the back of the doghouse, was a white ball of fur. The little hobo had come home!

The days passed and they heard nothing from the police or the pound. Denny and Randy were growing more and more anxious, because they could not bear the thought of having to give Sardo up. But they had noticed a hopeful sign. One day they had looked out the window and seen their dad playing with the dog. Sardo would jump onto his leg with all fours and then run around in a big circle as their dad engaged in a mock chase. Old-time salesmen often say that getting a prospect to touch the product is tantamount to making the sale; well, Sardo was doing one heck of a job selling himself. The next day their mom and dad took Sardo for a walk. This was getting better all the time!

And then the final week was up. Their dad was now playing with Sardo on his lunch hour, and their mom would join him for Sardo's evening walks. Actually, Denny and Randy were jealous of this, but they realized it was to their benefit to let it continue for a while. So it was that at the dinner table that night their dad, as he was buttering a slice of bread, casually remarked, "You can keep the dog." Denny and Randy jumped up screaming and ran out to tell Sardo, but he acted as if he already knew. A few weeks later, they asked their dad if he would sell Sardo for a million dollars, and he said no. If that wasn't true, it probably didn't miss by more than a few hundred thousand.

Sardo ("Sard" for short) quickly became a member of the family, although he wasn't allowed inside the house for many months. All he knew was that everyone in the family disappeared through the backdoor at night and re-appeared from it in the morning, and he couldn't stand to think that something was going on in there that he wasn't party to. He'd stand by the door and bark and whine as only a puppy can, and when he got no response he'd sulk off under a tree and look highly insulted.

One day Denny's mom and dad decided to let Sardo in the house for a few minutes to see how he would act. After all, they had no way of knowing if he had ever been inside a human house before. They opened the backdoor and called him. He came running and stopped abruptly at the threshold, even though the door was wide open for him. Old habits die hard.

"Come on, Sard," they urged. He looked at them as if to say, "Are you quite sure about this?"

"Sard, come on!"

Now he knew they were serious and he bolted in like a flash. He ran right through the den, through the living room, and came to a dead end in the kitchen. He made a skidding 180-degree turn on the linoleum floor and ran back through the living room and into the den. Turned on a dime and did the whole tour again at warp speed, ears pinned back flat on his head and barking like a machine-gun. And again. All you could see was a white streak every thirty seconds, like a comet with an extremely short interval.

After five minutes of this, they began to fear that he was going to self-destruct with a heart attack (or turn into a pool of butter), so they opened up the door and on his next return trip he ran right out into the yard and into his own house. And there he stayed, panting furiously.

As time went on, Sard's visits became less frenetic, until he was actually walking around the house with an air of sanity. He soon found a space behind the living room chair and made it his own. Eventually Sard began to spend as much time inside as out. He had full control over his schedule, barking at the door to come in and doing the same when he wanted out. But he never spent the night inside. At precisely 11:00 P.M. (this never varied by more than a few minutes), he would rouse himself from behind his chair, take a good long stretch, amble to the door, and bark to go out for the night. Once out he'd take a look around to make sure the world was as he'd left it, then retire into his private residence.

He even slept in his house during the dead of winter. Below-zero temperatures, blizzard conditions, he'd just curl up in the back of his house, snuggling in the blankets and hay Denny had put in for him. The colder it was, the better he seemed to like it. People who knew dogs guessed that he was part collie and part husky, and it must have been the latter that thrived in winter. But finally came a spell of record cold. The forecast was calling for a temperature of minus twenty-five degrees that particular night; they didn't know if Sard could withstand such conditions, though he seemed perfectly willing to try. They decided to keep him in for the night. It wasn't easy. He barked to go out at his usual time and everyone ignored him. He got mad and barked even louder.

They explained to him that it was for his own good, and then they all went to bed. He barked a few more times and then figured that if you can't beat them, you might as well join them. He jumped onto Denny's bed, walked over him in circles until he got it just right, and then collapsed with a sigh right over Denny's legs.

He did not spend another night outside for the rest of his life.

Sardo lived to the age of fourteen. He entered Denny's life when Denny was a kid and stayed until he was an adult. He chased around with Denny and his friends on the playground, got to know Denny's first girlfriend and others that followed (he loved them all), trusted Denny to drive him around when he first got his license, was there to greet him whenever he came home from college.

Finally it was time once again for Denny to leave for another school year. He packed his things as Sardo sadly watched. Sardo knew very well what suitcases meant. He lay down on the floor as Denny petted him good-bye. Sardo was old and suffering from the typical problems of a dog that age. Denny knew in his heart that it was probably the last time he would see him. He wondered if Sard knew that, too, because he didn't usually stay still that long to collect affection. He'd usually get antsy and go find something better to do. But not that day.

A few weeks later, Denny called home and engaged in the normal small talk. He waited until the last possible moment to ask what was really on his mind.

"Is Sard still around?"

"No," his mother said.

"I didn't think so. I've got to go. I'll talk to you soon."

Denny sat down at his desk, where a half-baked philosophy thesis was spread out, and cried.

And he thought how, for the most part, life passes by in a smooth continuum, one stage gradually and impercep- tibly becoming another, and you wonder how it was that you got to where you are. But then there are those times when you can literally feel part of your life breaking away, like a section of an iceberg cleaving off and sliding into the sea in a shock of noise and mist.

"No," his mother said.

Katrina, on the other hand, doesn't remember a time when her family didn't have dogs around. In rural Alabama, multiple dogs on and around the porch are required by the state building code. Over time, the cast of doggy charac- ters changed as pups were born, given away, strays ap- peared and stayed, dogs wandered off and didn't come back. They all were fed and sometimes played with, and in especially bad weather they were sheltered in the cellar.

Usually one dog would stand out and become "Katrina's dog." She had her heart broken many times when her favorite left her at much too young an age—country dogs face risks that we suburban dogs can't imagine! But for Katrina, there was never any doubt that there would always be another dog in her life.

After finishing college in the late 1980s, Katrina ven- tured north to take a job in upstate New York, the heart of "Yankeeland," and soon after arriving she met Denny. She taught Denny many things he didn't know. Example: each New Year's Day, to ensure prosperity for the coming year, you must eat black-eyed peas and hog jowl, along with a big ol' slice of cornbread. Example: it wasn't the "Civil

26

War"—it was the "War of Northern Aggression." However, because none of Denny's ancestors had even made it to America until well after that bloody misunderstanding, Katrina felt that it would not be traitorous to date Denny. As for Denny, it wasn't long at all before he found himself breaking all of Doc's rules again.

Katrina was happy, but for two things: she was cold all the time (the Fourth of July was the only exception) and she had no dog. Denny explained that since they both worked there was no way they could have a dog and be fair to it. And they liked to travel to foreign countries—how could that continue with a dog? (He knew that once he had a dog he wouldn't be able to bring himself to board it—smart guy!)

After a few years, frostbite had finally lost its charm, even for Denny. They shoveled their cars out one last time, moved to Sarasota, Florida, got married, and bought a house. With the preliminaries dispensed with, certainly now they could get a dog! But Denny wouldn't budge. Undaunted, Katrina started visiting pet stores and dragging Denny with her. He loved the puppies just as much as she did, but there was no moving him on what was getting to be a very sore subject.

So Katrina continued to visit the pet shops on her own, leaving the impossibly cruel sourpuss at home. Then one day lightning struck: Katrina was in a pet store and behind the glass she saw a puppy that moved her to tears. It was the most beautiful, loveable little creature she had ever seen. Katrina put her hand up to the glass and the puppy tried so hard to lick her fingers. An employee brought the puppy out for Katrina to hold, and she couldn't believe she could instantly love something so profoundly.

Of course, this dog was a papillon! Katrina sat and held the dog for as long as she dared. It was so hard to leave the store without that little life cuddled next to her. She hurried home to tell Denny what had happened. As Katrina told the story, he knew that another round was about to begin and he sensed that this time Katrina was going for the knockout. She made him promise that he would go see the dog, but he kept on finding excuses to put it off. Meanwhile, Katrina visited the pup every day after work, terrified that he would still be there and terrified that he wouldn't.

One morning, after Katrina had left for work, Denny passed by her closet and something tucked way back in the corner caught his eye. It was a plastic shopping bag with what appeared to be a tiny basketball in it. He opened the bag and almost passed out. It contained a little toy basketball, a plastic bone, and a leash and collar. He had only one hope—Christmas was approaching and maybe, just maybe, Katrina had gotten these as gifts for someone else's dog.

He grabbed the phone and called her at work.

"Katrina, you know that plastic bag in your closet, the one with the doggy stuff in it? Who's that for?"

Dead silence.

"Katrina, you know that plastic bag way back in your closet, the one with all the doggy toys in it? Who's that for?"

Even deader silence.

Denny was now dizzy. He sat down.

"Katrina, you didn't get that stuff for the dog you know you can't have, did you?"

"I couldn't help it."

And that was it. The thought of poor Katrina wandering around the store, picking out toys for a dog that wasn't to be, melted his heart. Further opposition was useless. Later that day he purchased a book on papillons, and when Katrina got home from work he gave it to her. He told her that the only way he could imagine himself consenting to get a dog was to find a plastic bag filled with doggy toys in her closet. (And Denny could not help remembering what Doc had taught him so long ago about the relative intelligence of men and women.) They would get a dog, it would be a papillon, and it would have to come from a breeder. And the project was all Katrina's.

Before long, she had networked her way around the country by phone and the Internet, learning about the breed, going to dog shows, talking to experts, and filling up a notebook with names and addresses of breeders, none of whom had anything available. She persisted for many weeks, refusing to become discouraged. Then a breeder from Georgia mentioned that she had heard through the papillon grapevine that there were several puppies for sale by a breeder in Venice, Florida. Was that anywhere near Katrina? Ten whole miles, that's how near. Another phone call, a pleasant chat with a friendly lady named Sharon, and soon Katrina found herself sitting on the floor, dragging the cutest little puppy in the world out from under the chair.

Then she rushed home to tell Denny that she had found exactly what she was looking for.

Me.

3

My New Home

A few days after Katrina's first visit, she was back again and this time she brought Denny. Katrina got down on the floor and played with me like before, while Denny sat off to the side and watched. He was very quiet. He seemed dazed.

Eventually he regained consciousness and started to play with me and Hunter and Heidi. But he seemed to be paying more attention to Hunter than to us girls. I hate it when I'm not the center of everyone's world. *I'll show him*, I thought. So I started chasing Emma and Cecily around and nipping their butts. This seemed to make him laugh (humans have a weird sense of humor), and then he said something to Sharon. I didn't know much English then, but I heard the word "deposit" and he handed her some green paper. I wanted to chew it up, but Sharon put it into a drawer. Finally, Denny and Katrina left, and that was no skin off my nose.

On the way home, Denny explained to Katrina that he had really wanted a male dog because he felt that he would be able to relate to him better. Male dogs were tougher and you could roughhouse with them, he said, whereas females were delicate and you had to treat them more gently. (Keep in mind that this brilliant opinion came from someone who had never owned a female dog.) But when Denny saw me putting on my show, chasing the big dogs around while Hunter fell asleep, I won his heart. Doc needs to add an important corollary to his principles: the dumbest female dog is smarter than the smartest man!

I had no idea what I had done by impressing Denny so; I just wanted attention and admiration. If I had gone to sleep like Hunter did, I might still be living at Sharon's.

By Florida law, a breeder cannot release a puppy before it is eight weeks old, so Katrina had two weeks to get her house ready for me. She also had to think of a new name for me. I knew I wasn't really a "Hannah" and she knew it, too. Sharon had just given me a temporary name, fully expecting it would be changed by my new owner. But what was my real name? Katrina started looking through name books, searching through the dictionary, trying out different possibilities both in her head and aloud, looking for a name that had the magic ring of truth. She wasn't finding it.

One night she settled down with a guidebook to Paris. After all, she loved Paris and "papillon" was as French as you could get. Somewhere in that book she knew she'd find the answer. Let's see. "Madeleine"? "Marly"? "Chapelle"? "Passy"?

No.

"Eustache"? "Vivienne"? "Lille"? "Marguerite"?

Not even close.

She kept turning pages. Then her eyes landed on a sentence: "The patron saint of Paris is Saint Genevieve." *Genevieve!* That was it, without a doubt. That had been my real name all along! Katrina was so excited that she dropped the book and ran to tell Denny.

Denny was in the kitchen making one of his gross concoctions for supper. Katrina has a style of eating that dictates that separate food items be placed on the plate without touching and are under no circumstances to be mixed, or chewed, together. Each type of food should remain pure and unadulterated, so that its unique essence can be enjoyed without distraction.

Denny is from the other school. When Katrina arrived in the kitchen, out of breath with excitement, he was in the process of pouring raisins into the noodles he was cooking. She knew from experience that this horror would eventually be mixed with cottage cheese, cinnamon powder sprinkled on top, and consumed with a side of applesauce. But for now she would overlook this stomach-churning excuse for nourishment because she had such wonderful news.

"I found our puppy's name!"

"Good. What is it?"

"Genevieve!"

"What?"

"Genevieve."

"You can't name a dog 'Genevieve.'"

"Why not?"

"Every reason. For one thing, it's too much of a human name. It just doesn't go with a dog. For another, it's too long. It weighs more than the dog does. It's three syllables. You need a one- or two-syllable name for a dog. You can't be out in the yard yelling, 'Gen-e-vieve,' 'Gen-e-vieve.'"

Katrina felt as though Denny had just doused her with a tub of ice water. How could a man who was about to ingest that hideous mess express a negative opinion on anything?

"I don't believe you," Katrina said. "It's perfect. It's her name. If you can come up with something better, let me know." She paraded out of the kitchen.

"I will," he said, as he mixed orange juice and grape juice together to drink with his meal.

Katrina stewed for days. Several times she saw Denny leafing through the French dictionary, but he didn't seem to be enjoying any "eureka experiences." Finally, without any preface at all, he announced: "I give up. You can name the dog 'Genevieve.' Maybe it's not so bad." In truth, he was struggling mightily with the image of himself walking a three-pound ball of white fluff named Genevieve through the neighborhood. Maybe he'd have to buy a big Harley to offset this. But he didn't know how to ride one.

Meanwhile, I had all but forgotten about Katrina and Denny when they showed up at Sharon's again one evening. Katrina sat down in the middle of the living room floor and smiled at me. This time I kept my distance because I smelled some kind of big trouble brewing.

"Genevieve," she said, "C'mere Genevieve."

My ears shot straight up and I felt a shock of excitement. How did she know my real name? No one else seemed to know it. I ran over and licked her hands, and she picked me up and smothered me with kisses and hugs.

"Did you see that?" exclaimed Katrina with a note of triumph. "She came running right over as soon as I said her name." Denny could only shake his head, starting to feel outnumbered by us girls already.

Then things started happening fast. Denny gave Sharon some more green paper and Katrina attached something she called a "leash" to my collar. Sharon hugged and kissed me and said, "Good-bye, Genevieve, I'll miss you."

What do you mean "good-bye"? Where are you going, Sharon?

Katrina picked me up and started walking out the door with me. Wait a minute! This was going a little too far! "Mommy, Mommy!" I barked, but Chloe just looked at me sadly as she sat in the corner, as if she knew she could do nothing to stop this puppynapping. Then they carried me into a car and started off. I had only been in a car a couple of times before, when Sharon had taken us puppies to the vet for a checkup and some nasty stick things. I was so scared that I was breathing really fast and whimpering, too. Katrina and Denny kept telling me that everything was OK, but when they pulled onto I-75 I knew I was in a world of hurt. I'd heard the big dogs say that once you got onto I-75, there was no telling where you might end up.

We hadn't gone too far when we got off the big road and started going slower, and soon we pulled into a garage.

Katrina carried me into the house and put me down. "Welcome home, Genevieve."

"Pick me back up!" I yelled. First of all, I hate linoleum floors and, second, who knew what monsters were lurking just around the corner of this strange house. Katrina picked me up and carried me around, showing me each room. I didn't care much for the decor; it was too dark for my taste. Then they took me for a walk around my new neighborhood. As near as I could smell, there were seven dogs, three cats, a rabbit family, and a snake in the area. I left my mark in as many places as I could, just to let them all know there was a new sheriff in town.

A little later it was bedtime. Now, get this. Katrina put me in a plastic box with bars on the front, set the box in the corner of the bedroom, and then they both climbed into a nice warm bed. My whole life, all two months of it, I'd gone to sleep cuddled up with my family. Now, just who was the genius that thought I would be happy with this new arrangement? I started screaming as loud as I could. I found that the plastic box I was in made a great echo chamber, with the bulk of the sound conveniently aimed directly at Denny and Katrina.

They tried to talk to me and tell me to go to sleep, but I was a dog on a mission. After an hour, Katrina got up and released me from prison. She carried me into the living room and lay down on the couch with me, covering us both with a blanket. This was more like it. I fell asleep in her arms and slept soundly until 5:00 A.M., when I decided that everyone had slept long enough and that it was PLAYTIME.

After a short walk in the darkness and a ten-minute play session, I went back to sleep, leaving Denny and Katrina wide-eyed and exhausted.

Not a bad start.

4

A Period of Adjustment

The next few weeks were hard for me. I learned my way around the house, but I didn't dare go into a room by myself. I hadn't heard or smelled any monsters, but one can't be too careful these days. I kept looking for Chloe and the rest of my family, but they weren't there. Was I doomed to spend the rest of my days with only humans for companions? That prospect was so depressing that I lost my appetite and refused to eat unless Denny or Katrina fed me by hand. This was actually part of my master plan to show them right from the beginning who was the boss. If you let humans think they have the upper hand, they can be a nightmare to live with.

I had lots of other tricks, too. If they tried to pet me I nibbled on their fingers. I would never come when they called me; I trained them to give me a treat if they wanted me to get close enough to put the leash on. I especially liked going pee-pee or poopy on their nice beige carpet when they weren't looking. It was so much fun to watch them discover it and then go running around, grabbing paper towels and sponges and funny-smelling cleaner stuff. I'd go over to the mess and sniff it and look up at them as if to say, "What lowlife could have done this to our beautiful home?" Sometimes I think my acting job was so good that they began to suspect each other.

Another way I tormented them was by getting the "zooms." This is where I would run around and around the living room at one hundred miles an hour, for no apparent reason. It was so exciting that sometimes I'd poop in midair without even meaning to. They had never seen a dog get the zooms before, and they were convinced that either I had a serious medical problem or had allowed the devil to take up residence in my body.

I also continued making Katrina sleep with me at night on the couch. Finally, in desperation, she moved my plastic prison cell close to the bed, and when I'd start whining she'd put her hand down next to the bars where I could nuzzle it. That made me feel a little better, so I eventually accepted those sleeping arrangements for the time being. But I knew it was only temporary because my ultimate goal was to ascend to my rightful position up on that bed.

As time went on and I gained confidence, I began to explore the house on my own and found it to be monster-free. It got so that Katrina or Denny often didn't know what room I was in and, of course, I wouldn't come when they called me. They had to look under every chair, table, sofa, and bed in the house in order to find me. I thought that was just too funny! They eventually got smart and started closing the doors to all the rooms, so that I was limited to the living room and the kitchen. But if I had to be stuck in one room for the rest of my life, it would definitely be the kitchen, because I've learned that's where all the good stuff happens. Here is my list of the good stuff, starting with the Absolute Best and working down to Very Delicious:

1. Pizza
2. Pizza
3. Pizza
4. Chicken
5. Steak
6. Cheese
7. Eggs
8. Pasta
9. Tuna
10. Baked Potato

I also can't resist doggy cookies and treats. Unlike the foods on the above list, which are to be eaten as rapidly as possible to prevent possible theft, I like to play with cookies and treats before I eat them. I bat them around the room with my paws and fling them into the air with my teeth. Then I watch them out of the corner of my eye and pounce on them when they least expect it. Denny says this is good training in case I have to catch my own cookies someday.

I hate dry dog food. The dog food companies spend big money every year trying to develop a dry food that will be irresistible to us dogs, and yet on any given day I find ten dead things outside that taste better. Denny just loves it when I spit out his ten-buck-a-bag dog food and then gobble down a sun-baked, crushed lizard I find in the road. Humans don't seem to appreciate that natural is better; I haven't seen Katrina or Denny eat anything off the road yet, and there has been some terrific stuff out there.

One of my favorite activities in the whole world is wrestling with Denny. We get on the couch and Denny pushes me over onto my back, and I start kicking him and biting his fingers. Katrina is always telling Denny not to wrestle with me because she says it's really a struggle for dominance and I'm winning. This seems to be a characteristic of humans: they're always looking for the "real" reason we dogs do things. Listen to me. Sometimes we chew on the curtains, not because we're bored, but because they're waving around, making fun of us. Sometimes we poop on the rug, not because we're mad at you, but because we're in a hurry and it's so convenient. And sometimes I wrestle with Denny, not to prove anything, but just for fun.

But most of the time it's to show him who's boss.

Sometimes I lie on the couch with Denny or Katrina and watch TV. They seem to like different kinds of shows. Denny watches men running around, knocking each other over while they chase a ball. I think they're trying to play doggy football, but they're not very good; humans can't run fast at all, because they're stuck with only two legs. And they carry the ball in their arms instead of their teeth, like they should. Katrina watches shows where men and women are always kissing each other, while soft music plays. And there's always an old, ugly woman with pulled-back hair who's trying to cause trouble for everybody. Nobody kisses her.

My favorite programs are the ones about wolves. When they show the mother wolf taking care of her babies it reminds me of my mommy, Chloe, and me. I get so excited that I jump right in front of the TV and start to whimper. When the wolves put their heads back and howl, I do it, too. At first, for reasons I'll never be able to figure out, Katrina and Denny thought this was hysterically funny. But then Katrina started to catch on, and now she does it with me. Her accent is bad, but the spirit is right. When we both get going, Denny leaves the room. I think he might be scared.

I fell in love with a puppy on my block. His name is Barli. He's a Bernese mountain dog, weighs 175 pounds, and is still growing—why, I don't know. When I first saw him I thought he was a car with fur. Denny and Katrina held me up so I could kiss him all over his face. But when he opened his mouth to grin at me, I was afraid I was going to fall down into that big hole. Since then, Barli has learned to lie down flat on the ground so I can walk around him and kiss him on my own. I still have to be careful, though. One time he lifted up his paw to greet me and knocked me for a loop. Barli is so strong that his humans attach a cart to him and let him pull children around at fairs. I want Barli to pull me in that cart to our wedding. Everyone keeps telling me that I have to stick to my own kind; they don't understand that this is not puppy love. But right now, Denny and Katrina keep a close eye on me. Sometimes I don't think they trust me with boys.

After I had lived with Denny and Katrina for a couple of months, they took me back to Sharon's for a visit. I think they were a little apprehensive that once I saw my family again I wouldn't want to go back home with them. Chloe was so excited to see me that she showered me with kisses. Heidi and Hunter were gone; I guess they had moved away to new houses, too. The cat was uglier than ever. Cecily had missed me terribly, and she wanted to run and play with me. The problem was old lemonface Emma; she had become a real bitch since I'd left. She didn't seem to like it that I was back and getting so much attention; she was acting just like those mean ladies on Katrina's shows. She started to growl at me, but Chloe jumped on her and told her to mind her manners. When I get bigger I'm going to have a little talk with Emma.

Sharon kept on hugging me and telling me what a pretty girl I had become. I already knew that, but there was no harm in letting her blather on about it for a bit. It also made Emma even madder, which was good.

We stayed for an hour, and then it was time to go. I kissed Sharon and Chloe and Cecily good-bye, and gave the cat and Emma the doggy equivalent of the bird. (This involves looking at your victim out of the corner of your eye and flicking your tail out straight for a few seconds.) In spite of Denny and Katrina's fears, I didn't mind leaving at all. There was too much competition in that house for ruler of the roost. I much preferred my new home, where I was the undisputed queen.

How could I have known that even then dark forces were hatching a plot to rob me of my power?

5

Elementary Education

Looking back at it now, I have to admit that I was turning into a bit of a juvenile papliquent, and I was really giving Denny and Katrina all they could handle. I continued to chew on their fingers whenever they tried to pet me. I didn't want anything to do with the food they gave me; I wanted theirs. When they called me, I just sat and stared at them. If they tried to put the leash on me to take me out, I ran the other way. I much preferred doing my business on the nice clean rug, instead of on that damp, dirty grass outside. To sum it all up, if there was going to be a pack consisting of some humans and me, I was going to lead it.

Denny would ask Katrina: "How can it be that a 170-pound, full-grown man, with all the accumulated wisdom of thousands of years of human history, can't control a three-pound, four-month-old puppy?" Katrina, who normally has all the answers whether Denny asks for them or not, seemed stumped on this one, too.

They started bringing home books by the dozens on raising and training dogs. I don't know who writes these books, but if I had been their puppy they would have given up their author dreams within hours. At various times, I was put in my crate when I was bad, reprimanded in stern tones while they looked at me directly in the eyes, rewarded with a treat when I pretended to willingly do what they wanted, ignored, screamed at, and clicked at by a stupid little gadget Katrina ordered. All of this gave me ample opportunity to practice my heartbreaking whine and my "why-are-you-so-mean-to-me?" head-cocked-to-the-side, forlorn little expression.

One day, while I was hiding, Katrina got on the phone and started asking about "trainers." This was going to be interesting. I liked it when they tried something new. Later that evening, Katrina put me on her knees and, as I nibbled away at her fingers, said, "Genevieve, Judy is coming to the house tomorrow to teach you how to be a good dog."

Oh, this was going to be so good! Another human who thought she could deal with me. *Bring her on*, I thought. I was so excited I could hardly sleep that night; I barked and whined for hours so that Katrina and Denny couldn't either.

Late the next afternoon the doorbell rang. I started screaming and carrying on even worse than usual. I was going to intimidate this Judy even before she got in the house. Denny opened the door and Judy came in. Judy was big, a lot bigger than Katrina. Bigger than Denny, too. I jumped at her legs a few times and nipped at her shoes. I wanted to scare her, but not so bad that she would leave before I had a chance to really work her over. I smelled a lot of dogs on her: German shepherds and Chinese cresteds and poodles and dogs I didn't even recognize. I guess none of them had had what it takes to put Judy in her place. Don't worry guys, Genevieve's here now. We're going to retire Judy from the dog business.

Judy walked over to the dining room table and sat down. She was carrying some kind of metal case, which she put on top of the table. I really wanted to know what was in that case, but I'd leave that for later.

Judy called for me to come. I sat ten feet away and stared at her. She called me again. I looked over at Denny and Katrina. Hadn't they told Judy about me? Was this woman kidding?

Then Judy asked Denny and Katrina to put the leash on me. I made them chase me all over the room before they were able to corner me and get the leash on. I fought for all I was worth. I wanted to put on a really exciting show for Judy so she could see exactly what she was dealing with.

Denny brought the leash over and gave it to Judy. She called me and then started to drag me toward her. My little butt was getting a rug-burn! Then she picked me up. OK, welcome to my world, Judy. I started chewing on her hands extra hard. I was going to introduce her to a new friend— pain.

Wait a minute. Her hands didn't taste right. Ooooo, they tasted so bad I wanted to barf. What's with this woman, anyway? Let some other sucker chew on those stank hands. I didn't want any part of them. Time to change the game plan. I started kicking and clawing with all fours. Then she did something I just couldn't believe. She grabbed me and lifted me way up in the air, with my little legs dangling straight down. Was this nutcase going to drop me or something?

I glanced over at Katrina and Denny. They looked as scared as I was. Hey, come and save me from this Terminator. But they didn't budge.

I stopped struggling. I was afraid I was going to kick myself right out of her grip. I didn't know if they made parachutes for dogs, but as soon as this was over I was going to look into it. Then she put me back on her lap and tried to pet me. Big mistake, lady. Take that. Don't worry, that shouldn't leave much of a scar.

Whoa, back up in the air. I just knew she was going to drop me now. Denny, Katrina—save me!

All right, all right, I'll be good. She put me back on her lap and started petting me. It gave me the creeps, but I thought that maybe if I kept calm she'd disappear. She put me down on the carpet and called to me. All right, I'll come, just get lost, please?

Then she picked me up and (I can hardly stand to talk about this even now) she cuddled me and put her cheek on my face. That was totally over the limit, so I started kicking like a rodeo horse on speed. Whomp! She tightened her hands around me and held me so firmly that I couldn't move. I felt like I was in some kind of doggy vise. Struggling was useless, so I just went limp. Do whatever you want, kiss me, cuddle me, just get it over with and HIT THE BRICKS.

I looked over at Denny, and he had an expression of amazement on his face.

"I can't believe it, Judy. We've tried everything, and you walk in and within two minutes she's a different dog."

That's right, Jack, because your hands don't taste like rotten shrimp (I hate shrimp!), and you don't dangle my delicate little body in midair, and you don't clutch me like a lovesick boa constrictor.

Now Judy was showing off, making a big production out of the fact that she had total command over me. Denny and Katrina were speechless as they watched me come when called, sit still to get petted, and lie totally limp in Judy's arms as she hugged me, scratched behind my ears, turned me on my back, and rubbed my tummy.

Finally the Warlord put me down. I scampered over to my lounging pillow and lay down, trying to recover from what had just happened. But I also wanted to keep an eye on The Incredible Hulk, just in case she picked up Denny or Katrina and made their legs dangle in the air.

Then she opened up her metal case and took out a plastic bottle of something she called "Bitter Apple." I perked up— maybe it was something for me to eat? Denny sprayed some on his hands and came over to pet me. Did he really think that just because I had allowed Attila the Hun to torture me that I was going to lie there and let him abuse me, too? I went to work on his fingers, like old times.

Wait a minute! Wait. WAIT JUST A DARNED MINUTE! No! No, no, no! Denny's hands tasted just like old Frankenstein's over there. It's the stuff in that bottle! And now Katrina is putting the bottle in the cupboard.

They're keeping it! Someone, please tell me this is all just a nightmare.

Godzilla finally left. But the damage had been done. Denny and Katrina both had rotten-shrimp hands. And now they kept the leash on me all the time so they could retrieve me anytime they wanted. And when Katrina picked me up and I started kicking, she dangled me in the air.

I was a whipped pup. I had woken up only a few hours earlier the leader of the free world, and now it looked like I was going to have no choice but to be a ... a ... owwww it gives me the creeps just to say it. A SWEET dog.

The worst day of my entire life, no doubt about it.

Several months went by as I adjusted to my eroded authority. Since I never knew when Denny and Katrina were going to have puke hands, I generally left their fingers alone. And, since I now had to drag the leash around with me all day long, which meant that they could catch me whenever they wanted, I reluctantly came whenever they called me—a real downer!

They took me outside every few hours so that I wouldn't have what they called "an accident." I never could understand why my accidents caused such a fuss—Denny and Katrina have accidents in the house all the time. I know this because whenever they go into those little rooms, I scratch and bang on the door until they let me in and I always see them having an accident. They don't seem to understand one of the most basic of papillon rules: humans must not under any circumstances close a door with a papillon on the other side. We need to be sure that you're not making a sandwich, or playing with some other dog you sneaked in, or taking a nap without us.

One day I was looking out the window next to the front door and it looked so pretty out. The sun was shining and the wind was blowing the green grass back and forth, and I realized that I wanted to go pee-pee out there. Without even thinking, I barked. Denny jumped up and came over and saw me standing in front of the door. He got so excited it was pitiful.

"You need to go out, Genevieve?"

He grabbed the leash and out we went. I ran over to my favorite spot and squatted.

"Good girl, Genevieve, that's a good girl."

As soon as we got back in the house, he rushed over to the telephone and called Katrina. I couldn't make out everything he was saying, but I kept on hearing "she did it, she did it."

Hmmm. Maybe I was on to something here. I went over to the door and barked.

Denny dropped the phone and ran over to me.

"Do you have to go potty good girl?"

And out we went. I marched around sniffing the scenery for ten minutes while Denny sweated in the hot Florida sun. He finally gave up and brought me back inside.

A few minutes later I barked again. Now Denny seemed annoyed.

"Genevieve, I've had you out twice already. You don't have to go potty."

I gave a little whine. Back out we went. And I realized that now I had them both right where I wanted them. I could go outside anytime I wanted just by barking and whining at the front door. Maybe I had to do some business, maybe I didn't, but they couldn't afford to take the chance of ignoring me.

I made Denny take me out fifteen times that afternoon. I was back in charge!

It was about this time that Katrina and Denny began telling me that I was going to start school. I didn't know what school was, but there was something about the sound that I didn't like. Yet, I was hopeful—maybe they had pizza there. Then, one evening, they grabbed my leash and said, "C'mon, Genevieve, we're going to school." We piled into the car and, as usual, I helped Katrina drive, even though I didn't know where we were going.

We turned down a gravel road and stopped next to a big field. What I saw there made me go nuts: dogs everywhere, all walking on-leash with their humans, up and back, around and around. Big dogs and small dogs, longhaired and shorthaired. I had never seen so many dogs in one place in my whole life. I loved school!

"Let me out, let me out!" I yelped. Denny and Katrina were taking too darned long getting their things together. I was going to be late for school! Katrina finally opened the door and I dragged her out of the car.

"Hurry, hurry, hurry." I wanted to join the party and play.

But, wait—something was wrong. Everyone was so quiet. The dogs weren't talking to one another, and neither were the humans. Most of the dogs were acting very strange.

They were walking alongside their humans and following their every step. They weren't sniffing the grass, or digging holes, or darting this way and that. Were they sick or something?

Katrina was pulling me to the other end of the field, where there were tables and chairs and more humans. Wait a minute. Who was that big woman holding that weird thing in front of her mouth that seemed to make her voice louder than it should be? Something familiar there. Hmmm. Let's get a little closer. Oh, no! No! Please, it can't be.

IT'S JUDY!

Oh, gosh, take me home. Not this again. I hate school!

I looked around and saw Denny sitting in a chair at the edge of the field. Couldn't he see what was happening here? Didn't he love me anymore? All the dogs and humans were gathering in front of General Patton. I had an idea. If I hid behind Katrina's leg, maybe Tyrannosaurus Rex wouldn't notice me.

Across the field boomed: "Hello, Katrina, I'm glad you could make it. If you don't mind, please bring Genevieve up here. I want to demonstrate something to the class."

My cover was blown before I even started. No way could she have seen me. Someone must have ratted me out. I felt like a condemned prisoner taking that last walk. We got to the front and King Kong grabbed me and picked me up. As I dangled there, I looked out at the other dogs. There was pity in their expressions. And gratitude that it was me, instead of them.

"Class, this is Genevieve, and she's an eight-month-old papillon." Eight and a half, dimmo.

"Several months ago Katrina called me for a personal training session because she and her husband felt that they had no control over Genevieve, and nothing that they were trying seemed to work." Oh, yeah, the good old days.

"So I went over to work with Genevieve for a session. Don't let her small size fool you. Genevieve is what I call a tough dog." Hey, I like that.

"But by applying the proper training techniques, Katrina tells me that she's a different dog now." Right, I refuse to chew on barfola fingers, I freeze up at 10,000 feet, and I come whenever someone calls my name and drags me across the floor by my leash.

"And I'm sure she's going to do just fine in our obedience class." Yes, I'm sure, too. Now put me down and go give a speech to Congress.

"Now I want to demonstrate how to put on a choke chain, so since I have little Genevieve up here I'll use her."

It didn't matter any more. I knew then that this woman would never run out of ways to torment me. A choke chain! There wasn't even the feeblest attempt to cover over the reality with a nice-sounding name like "training collar." Or "corrective neckwear." Or "obedience aid."

Choke chain. She slipped this relic from the Inquisition over my head and told me to sit. I didn't care what it cost me; I was going to embarrass her in front of the whole class. I just stood there admiring the pretty clouds. She yanked on my leash. I suddenly realized that breathing was just a memory, and I banged my butt onto that grass so hard I could have driven a railroad spike. I figured it was a standoff. I had made my point and she had made hers.

Every week for the next two months I had to go to school. The lessons included how to sit, stand, deck (lie down), stay, come, and heel. By the time we got to the final exam, I could do all those things perfectly. It was just that most of the time I didn't want to. And I didn't want to during the final exam. I tugged at the leash when I was heeling; I didn't sit until Katrina told me three times; and instead of staying down for the required three minutes, I jumped up after thirty seconds. Something was tickling me and I just had to scratch it.

Poor Katrina was so nervous. She looked like she was going to cry each time I screwed up. Denny was sitting in his chair, laughing. Sometimes I think he likes it when I show my independent streak.

After all the dogs had finished the test, we lined up for the graduation ceremony. None of us knew if we had passed or not. They started calling out the dogs' names, one by one, and each went up to get the diploma. Finally, they called my name, and Katrina broke out into a broad grin. She was so proud of me. Eventually, all of us got our diplomas and we ran around kissing and congratulating each other.

Before we left, Katrina took me up to Judy to thank her. Judy patted me on the head and told me that I had done very well and to keep it up. I wagged my tail a little, just to show that there were no hard feelings. Of course, there were, but I had decided that I would let her live.

OK, school's out—now get me out of here!

6

Dog and Driver

When Denny and Katrina first brought me home, I wanted no part of riding in a car. I didn't care what anybody said—I wasn't about to trust a room that moved. And once you got out on the highway, you had to contend with all those other moving rooms with people trapped in them. They were probably just minding their own business, watching television or eating dinner, when all of a sudden the room took off. I couldn't figure out why all those people weren't screaming right along with me.

But soon I began to realize that the car was the only room in the whole house that would move like that, and it only seemed to do it when Katrina or Denny sat in it and poked around for a few seconds. I started to get used to riding in the car, and then I grew to love it.

Many of my doggy friends hate riding in cars, just as I did. I hope that a few tips can turn automobile travel into a pure joy.

The first thing to keep in mind is that you are far safer riding in a car than you are trotting down the side of the highway on your own. You can be sure that all those poor creatures you see lying along the road were not riding in cars when they became a statistic.

The key to an enjoyable car ride resides in a few basics.

It is crucial that you sit in the driver's lap at all times. To insure that this happens, as soon as the car door is opened, jump onto the driver's seat and lie down. The driver will not be able to get in until he bends over and picks you up, and then the easiest thing for him to do is to sit down and put you on his lap. Other passengers may try to get you to sit in their laps, but pay no attention to them. As mere passengers they have no status. You are the only other soul in the car that can share the prestige of the driver's seat, so take full advantage of it.

When stopped at a light, I recommend looking out the window and trying to get the attention of the people in the cars alongside. Pretend to get very excited when they see you. If you do this well, the other drivers will be so intent on watching you and appreciating how cute you are that they won't notice when the light changes, and you will get a good head start on them. Little old ladies are most susceptible to this ploy, so save your best efforts for them.

Learning to recognize the sound of the blinker is an important element in riding in a car. When you hear that sound, it means that your driver needs your help in turning the steering wheel. Stand up with your back legs planted firmly in the driver's lap, and put your front paws over the top of the steering wheel. Learn how to shuffle your paws over the top of the wheel as it turns to keep from losing your balance. In this position you may very well block your driver's view of the road, so it is very important that you add just the right amount of steering input to help point the car in the right direction.

Whenever your driver stops the car and opens the window to talk to someone, you must act as if you want to kill that person. The reason is that in most cases he or she is about to take money from your owner, money that could have been spent on you. It is very important that you indicate in no uncertain terms just how mad this makes you, so that it won't happen again.

The one exception to this rule is when stopping at a drive-in bank window. This is for two reasons. One is that your owner may actually be getting money to spend on you, so let the bank humans do their job. Second, if you act like a sweet dog the bank human will often send out a biscuit for you. Because of this, do not let your owner bank by mail or use ATMs, because this way of doing business is totally unfair to dogs.

When you are riding in a car, all dogs that you see walking with their owners are deserving of your contempt, which is best expressed by an hysterical, siren-like bark as you pass by. It is up to you to decide whether or not to acknowledge the existence of other dogs riding in cars. If, unlike you, they are in the passenger seat, or even more pitiful, the back seat, it is perfectly appropriate to scream at them. However, if you see a dog riding in the back of a pickup truck, I would advise looking the other way.

First of all, these dogs are going to be in a bad mood because they're stuck riding outside, while you are getting to actually help drive the car. Moreover, these dogs tend to be a lot bigger and stronger than you, and if you make fun of them as you pass, you may bump into them again when you're out for a walk. If, however, the pickup has an out-of-state license and you're confident you'll never see them again, it is great fun to harass them as you go by. If you can get your owner to open the window far enough for you to stick your head out as you do this, it can be a showstopper.

Occasionally, you will see a human riding in a car that has been cut in half in some terrible accident, so that it has only two wheels. These cars have lost their tops as well. Most of these cars make a very loud noise, and they are usually driven by a 300-pound, bearded human named "Tiny." **DO NOT BARK AT TINY**.

Some of these cars don't make any noise at all, and their drivers have to make funny motions with their feet. They are usually driven by a scrawny guy named Marvin. Express your extreme disgust with Marvin by screaming at him as you go by. I have found that if you wait until your car is right alongside before you cut loose, you can often make Marvin's half-a-car tip over. This is one of the most gratifying things you will ever do.

Among the worst things you can ever see out on the roads is a cat perched on the shoulder of another driver. First of all, it is well known that cats can't drive a lick. So a cat in the driver's seat presents nothing but a hazard to every other car in the vicinity. And what motivates people to take a cat out in public where others can see it? Do they think it's funny? If you ever witness such a sight, get your owner to pull off the road until the danger has passed.

Something you never want to do in a car is throw up. Humans don't seem to like this. If you feel that you must, my advice is to do what I did: aim so that the barf goes down between the seats where it can't be seen. This eliminates the need for a big cleanup job, something your owner will appreciate.

If you follow these simple rules, you will always be a welcome guest in your owner's car.

7

Attending a Family Reunion

I knew something was up that morning when Katrina took all her clothes out of the closet and began to sort them on the bed. She does this every day when she's deciding what to wear to work, but this was different because Denny was doing the same thing with his clothes and he doesn't go to work. (Denny left his regular job in computer software shortly after I came home to live with him and Katrina. He told Katrina that he could make more money consulting, but Katrina knows that the real reason was so he could stay home with me. Denny vehemently denies this, but I can tell you that he plays with me all day long, and the only time he goes near the computer is when I make him take dictation for this book.) Denny's entire wardrobe consists of four T-shirts, two pair of shorts, and a large collection of jeans that don't fit. He seems to think that if he keeps the jeans hanging in the closet long enough they'll get larger. This is not working.

Then Katrina dragged out those big, soft boxes with the handles and zippers, and I knew that they were getting ready for a very long car ride, and I DAMNED SURE BETTER BE GOING, TOO. Just to make certain they hadn't forgotten about me, I followed them around the house wherever they went, attacking their heels. This is the best way I know for getting attention, and I don't understand why humans don't do it, too. Then Katrina went into the closet and pulled out my little travel bag, and I started zooming around the house. Yippee, I'm going on vacation!

Finally they got the car all packed and there was so much stuff that I was afraid there wouldn't be room for me. Katrina is not known as a light packer. In fact, I love when Denny tells the story about taking Katrina to Mexico for the first time. (This was before I was born, back when they thought they were happy.) He told Katrina to pack as light as possible because they would spend a lot of time carrying their bags around. When he leaned over to pick up Katrina's suitcase for the first time, he nearly left his arm attached to the handle. He asked her if she had packed a load of construction material. When they finally got to their destination, Katrina began to unpack. The first thing she pulled out was a metal flashlight several feet long, the kind that contains a thousand D batteries. Katrina won't repeat exactly what Denny said then, but I know him well enough to be sure what it was: "Are you [I don't understand this word] kidding me?"

Denny and Katrina made a final check of the house to be sure everything was turned off and all doors and windows were locked. And then we were off. Fifteen minutes later, they started remembering all the things they had forgotten. This is standard procedure for them. As soon as they have gone far enough so that returning to the house is out of the question, they suddenly remember dozens of things they should have brought. But they had remembered me, so the rest was their problem.

I helped Denny drive for about an hour, but I get bored driving on interstates (nothing to bark at) so I took a nap in his lap. After another hour they had to stop for the usual reasons: Denny was hungry and Katrina had to go pee-pee.

After I had several nice naps, we finally left the interstate and got on some Florida backroads that crawled through lots of small towns. I didn't like the way these places looked and I didn't like the people walking around in them. I yelled through the window at everything that moved. This seemed to work, because soon we'd be out in the countryside again, where I could relax.

Oh-oh, all of a sudden I got that queasy feeling—I knew I needed to go outside bad! I ran around the car but I couldn't find the front door to scratch at. Cars are stupid that way. We were in the middle of nowhere and there was no place to pull off the road. Denny got real worried and made the car go very fast. After a few minutes we saw a parking lot and a big field of grass. We stopped and Denny took me into the field, and I started an ambitious fertilization program.

Then a green car with writing on it pulled up, and a lady got out and came over to us. She was wearing funny green clothes with a shiny thing on her shirt and a big piece of metal strapped to her belt. She wasn't smiling like people do when they see how cute I am. She smelled mad.

She was telling Denny something. I couldn't understand it all, but it had something to do with being on the grounds of a prison and we had to get out of there. Denny was telling her that we couldn't help it, that his dog was sick. Just to help him out, I shifted my business end toward her and got back to work. She left in a huff, and Katrina and Denny started laughing. My quick thinking had kept them out of that prison.

After more naps than I can count, I heard Katrina say, "We're here! Mexico Beach, the Panhandle." We all tumbled out of the car. The air smelled salty and I could hear a strange roar. Katrina went into a little office to talk to some lady, and Denny took me for a walk over a hill. And then I saw a gigantic tub filled with water, with sand all along the edge as far as I could see. The water was moving up and down and making noise, and crazy white birds were flying all around, laughing at me and making me mad.

I wanted to run down and smell the water and dig in the sand and bite some of those birds, but Denny wouldn't let me go.

"Dogs aren't allowed on the beach," he said.

Oh, I see. Those birds can run all over it pooping to their hearts' content, and dead fish can lounge around and rot on it, and little crabby things can chase each other all over it, and humans can park their butts on it, BUT DOGS AREN'T ALLOWED. Well, I didn't drive all this way for nothing. You just wait and see where I take my walk to-night.

We walked back and Katrina was opening a door. I ran right in to check the scene out. Big living room, sniff sniff, kitchen, yeah, look at that bed, bounce bounce, bath-room, sofas and chairs, and I LIKE THIS PLACE. Time to take a nap on the sofa, while Denny drags in the two tons of stuff Katrina brought along. And that must be the flashlight Denny was talking about, except this time Katrina had packed two of them.

Once we got all our stuff moved in and Denny was exhausted, we got back in the car and drove down the road for a few minutes, until we came to another bunch of rooms. Katrina explained to me that we were going to meet her family, who had driven down from Alabama to meet us for the weekend. She knocked on a door and when we went in, people were everywhere: big ones and little ones and medium-sized ones. There was plenty of fuss going on, everyone kissing and hugging, and I just ran around and tried to get my share. I met Katrina's sire and dam, Murray and Emily, as well as her littermates, a brother, Ted, and sister, Becky. Becky had two girls: Halee, who was twelve, and Faith, who was four. They loved me. And Ted had a baby, Tristan, who was nine months old, just like me. Plus there were husbands, wives, and cousins—I gave up trying to figure out who belonged to whom.

I kept trying to lick Tristan because he smelled good, but they wouldn't let me. Human babies don't seem to have a bit of sense. All he did all weekend was lie around and suck on a bottle, and then have accidents in his little white pants. I had been only eight weeks old when I moved away from home to start my new life as Denny and Katrina's boss, so I couldn't understand why everyone was making such a fuss about Tristan. I'm cuter! Look at me, look at me!

I got along very well with Katrina's family because their schedule was just like mine: eat and sleep, eat and sleep. The two little girls, Halee and Faith, kept trying to pull me this way and that, but I was patient with them because I've learned that humans have to live for at least thirty years before they know anything.

Each night about midnight, Katrina and Denny took me for an illegal walk on the beach, and we had the whole thing to ourselves: no poopy birds or other humans to get in my way. I kicked sand all over the place, especially onto Katrina and Denny; since I was on a leash, I had them right where I wanted them. After our walk, it was bedtime. They hadn't brought along my nighttime crate, so they picked me up and put me on top of the bed, and then they went to sleep. So this is what it was like to sleep on a bed! It was just as I had imagined: plenty of room for me to find the perfect position, soft and warm. But not warm enough. I found a crack where the sheet started and burrowed my way under, right between Katrina and Denny. Now I was warm and safe, and I knew that I was never again going to settle for less. Katrina and Denny didn't realize it yet, but that nighttime crate back home had just become yard-sale material.

After several days of visiting, eating, and sleeping, we loaded up the car again and got back on the road. I knew we were in for a long ride, so a few minutes after we left I curled up on Denny's lap as he drove and started my first nap. All of a sudden, I heard Denny say a bad word and he made the car stop. I jumped up to see what was wrong. The window opened and this mean-looking man wearing silver sunglasses came walking up. And, oh no, he had one of those shiny things on his green shirt and a metal-thing on his belt! He must be from that prison, too. I started screaming at him to get away from us. He backed up and then Denny tried to give him some papers through the window. When the bad man tried to grab the papers, I almost jumped out of the window at him I was so ticked off.

The man backed up even farther and said something to Denny. Katrina grabbed me and Denny got out of the car. I jumped over to the back window and saw the man talking to Denny. I was howling mad—we'd been making good time until this fool ruined it.

The man and Denny were looking at me and laughing. Then the man gave Denny back the papers, got in his ugly car, and drove away. Denny came back and gave me a big hug. He told me that I was so cute that I'd saved him from a speeding ticket. He called me a "financial asset." I think that might be good.

We drove and drove, and after it got dark I saw the lights of our street and I started getting all excited. We got back in the house, and I ran around to make sure nobody had messed with my stuff while I was gone.

Hey, I think a tennis ball is missing! I know I had six and now I only count five. The heck with it. I'll look for it later. Time to take a nap.

Later that night, Denny and Katrina got ready for bed, and Katrina tried to get me to go into my crate. No way. I'll get back in that box when you sell that bed and sleep in a crate yourself. Until then, move over because here comes Genevieve.

The next day Denny put the crate in the garage; I'll let you know when they hold their sale.

8

Pet Peeves

As a papillon, I'm generally a happy, easygoing kind of girl. But there are some things that really get my dander up.

For example, I don't know how many times I've been in the middle of an important sleep research project when off goes the doorbell. Of course, I've got to protect my family by running to the door and sounding off at the top of my two-ounce lungs. Now, I'm not bragging or anything, but I can put out decibels worthy of an OSHA fine in an industrial setting. And though I now weigh only six pounds, Denny has said that if the best acoustical engineers in the world had to build a machine that was as loud as I am, it would weigh four tons. (I think that was a compliment.)

Anyway, there I'd be, preparing to chew my way through the door, when Denny and Katrina start laughing. This is just another example of how dense humans are.

Have you ever seen any of my four-legged colleagues laughing in the face of danger? No, we tend to business. Maybe we'll all sit around later and have a good laugh about how we treated that grizzly like lunch meat, but certainly not before.

And then come those humiliating words: "Genevieve, it's OK. It was just the TV."

Fooled again. Another darned commercial with a doorbell in it.

This is a waste of canine energy on a colossal scale. Every time a doorbell rings in a commercial, do you know how many dogs drop what they're doing and run barking to the door? Well, according to a study commissioned by the Society for the Prevention of Cruelty to Animals, it is 57,431. The collective wasted energy would be enough to fetch the morning newspapers of every American family for a month (not including the Sunday edition, which is so heavy that the labor laws should prohibit any dog from having to drag it in).

So I urge all my furry friends to write to the dogs in Washington and demand that doorbells be forbidden in all TV broadcasts.

Here's something that gets my hackles up: why aren't dogs allowed in government buildings? I even got kicked out of the local post office a few weeks ago. Katrina needed to get some stamps, but she didn't want to leave me in the hot car. So she carried me in her arms into the building and went to look at the stamp display. A sharp-eyed employee, no doubt suspecting that I was a bomb disguised as a little dog, promptly told Katrina we had to leave.

Oh, I get it—we dogs can die fighting for our country on the battlefield or helping the police keep the streets safer, but we're not wanted in your official buildings. I'm going to dog my congressman about this, too, you can bet on it.

I'll tell you something that makes my hair stand up on end: Denny sometimes tries to trick me so he can laugh at me. For example, he's too lazy to look for the clothes basket, so he carries his laundry back and forth in his arms. As soon as I see him do this, I follow him because he always drops at least one sock. When he does, I grab it and then the chase is on. Now, it's true, I do have some old socks in my toy box that Katrina and Denny gave me, but I have no interest in those. Like all dogs, I firmly believe that a toy given is fine, one stolen sublime.

Then one day Denny was carrying his laundry through the room and, as usual, he dropped a sock. But I just stared at it—something was fishy about the deal. And I was right; Denny had intentionally dropped one of my old socks, trying to con me into running off with it. If he knew how insulting such behavior was, he wouldn't do it anymore. But I guess he doesn't, because he does. He hasn't fooled me yet, and he never will. And now I get an even bigger thrill when I go running off with one of his sublime socks.

Another thing that puts a bug in my ear. When I go for a walk and I'm sniffing the ground, do you know what I'm doing? I'm reading a good story, that's what. I'm figuring out the who, what, when, where, and why. And sometimes, just as I'm getting to the final scene, Katrina or Denny yanks me by the leash and takes me home. And then I have to wait for my next walk so I can finish the story. And if it rains in the meantime, I never learn how it ends. It drives me crazy.

So I started doing the same thing to them. When Denny's watching humans trying to play doggy football on TV, I wait until the final minute, when he's on the edge of his seat. Then I go over to the front door and start whimpering. He pretends to ignore me. So I hunch over a little and flatten my ears. He moves fast then, puppy. And once we get outside, I take as long as possible to do my business. Then he runs back into the house, dragging me by all fours. And if I've timed it right, just as he opens the door we hear the announcer screaming, "That was the most unbelievable finish I've ever seen."

I do the same thing to Katrina when she's watching a cooking show. I do my little act just as the chef is explaining how long to cook the thing. One time, Katrina tried to bake a cake that she had seen on the program. But since I had tricked her into leaving the show at the crucial moment, she didn't know how long to bake it, and it exploded in the oven. I was hiding under the couch at the time, because I could smell it coming.

You have time for one more? I hate cats. Puppies often ask, "Why are there cats?" There is really no good answer for this. My personal opinion is that it was God's first attempt at making dogs and He screwed up. Big Time.

9

Going to the Doggy Supermarket

One of my favorite activities in the whole world is going to the doggy supermarket. It has a name, but I don't want to say it because Denny owns the stock and I don't want to jinx him. I really don't know what stocks are, but when the TV person says that they're down, Denny throws things and says words I don't understand.

I start going cuckoo as soon as we pull into the big parking lot. Denny or Katrina usually carries me into the store because of all the cars going every which way. I don't like that much, but being up high does give me a better view as I enter the store, and I can quickly see if there are any new displays I should know about. As we go through that creepy door (it opens even before we get there—how does it know? Can it smell us?), I like to announce my arrival by howling uncontrollably. This puts the other dog owners on notice to get their mutts out of my way, and it also alerts the cashiers to have a biscuit ready for me when we check out. They all know me, and they know that whenever I'm out on a shopping spree I don't cut anybody much slack.

As soon as Denny and Katrina put me down, I drag them by the leash to my favorite aisle, the toys. There are so many shapes and sizes and smells that I get overwhelmed trying to decide which ones I want. For some reason, Denny and Katrina won't let me chew on any of them. How am I supposed to pick something out without trying it first, like you humans do? For example, Katrina gets to try on all her clothes before she buys them. Then when she gets home she puts them on again and asks Denny if he likes them.

"Do you like this? Be honest," she always says.

"OK, I'll be honest. I don't really like it."

"What do you mean you don't really like it? What's wrong with it?"

"There's nothing wrong with it. I just don't like it."

"You don't know anything about clothes," Katrina says, as she stomps back to her closet.

A few minutes later she comes back out with something else on. "How about this? Be honest."

So since I don't get the chance to try out my toys first, Katrina and Denny always pick out ones for me that *they* like. I'm lucky I even get to play with my own toys at all. The one they seem to like the most, though, is my Kong toy. This is a hollow plastic tube, open at one end. When they bought it and gave it to me for the first time, I played with it for a few minutes and then got totally bored with it. After all, it doesn't have fur, it doesn't have a nose I can chew on, and it doesn't roll like a ball. *What a waste of my money*, I thought.

Then one night Katrina took Kong into the kitchen and was doing something to it on the counter. Now my curiosity was piqued. (Anything that goes on in the kitchen piques my curiosity.) She brought Kong back and put it on the floor. "Go get Kong," she said.

I went over and took a sniff. I felt like I had hit the mother lode—Kong was filled with peanut butter! Now I loved Kong and I settled down to clean it out. I was so busy that I didn't notice Katrina and Denny disappear into the bedroom. Normally I never let them go into any room unchaperoned, especially that one. It took me fifteen minutes to turn Kong back into its old boring self, and then I ran into the bedroom and jumped onto the big lump in the middle of the bed. Something wasn't right, because it was far too early for bedtime. They started laughing, as though they had put something over on me. I don't like that.

Since then, every once in a while they fill Kong up with peanut butter and disappear again. But now I've gotten so good that I can clean Kong out in five minutes. And when I fly onto the bed at the speed of sound, Denny has to go into the kitchen and fill Kong up again. A few days ago I made him get up twice to give me two Kong refills. I think this is good for him, because instead of lying in bed like that he should be getting more exercise.

After we leave the toy aisle, I like to browse in the food section. Denny and Katrina let me sniff at the boxes and cans to see my reaction. They don't seem to realize that all cans and boxes smell alike. So I just wag my tail at every-thing. Why don't they have people stationed around the store offering samples, like they do in human supermar-kets?

Katrina and Denny are always searching for a dry dog food that I'll eat. Of course, there is no such thing. I like to play a mean trick. Every few weeks they come home with another sample of dry food for me to try. And I just take a deep breath and gobble it up. They get all excited and im-mediately rush out to buy a big bag of the barfola. When they put it in my bowl I take one sniff and walk away. If I'm feeling especially bitchy, I'll gingerly take one piece in my mouth and then spit it across the room as if they had just fed me something from a toxic waste dump.

I'm hoping that after they waste enough money buy-ing food I won't eat, they'll finally accept the fact that all I really want for dinner is PIZZA.

Sometimes, after we get through the food section, they drag me into the cat, bird, and fish area of the store. It gives me the creeps—who would want those things living in the house with them, when they could have a dog like me? I would give anything to be able to poop or pee in that sec-tion to show the management what I think of their retail mix, but I can't because Katrina and Denny always make sure I go before we get in the store.

When we're in the cashier line I like to see the stuff other dogs are checking out. You wouldn't believe the junk food some of them buy. They usually look like they haven't chased a cat in years. And I hate those dogs that try to sneak more than ten items through the express lane, and then they make their owners write a check and take up even more of my valuable time. It's even worse in the wintertime, when all the elderly tourist dogs are here in Florida on vacation. They walk slowly, they can't see, and they certainly can't drive. Why don't they stay up north where they belong?

As we're leaving the store, I like to sneak a peek through the big window into the grooming area. I've seen some mighty cute guys getting their hair cut in there. To show off I'll bark at them, and then all the dogs get excited and try to jump off the grooming tables and cause a general commotion. I love to stir up trouble. I don't know why I'm like that. Do you think it was something that happened to me when I was a puppy?

10

Modern Medicine

If Katrina and Denny love me so much, why do they insist on dragging me to the vet? They seem to watch me constantly, looking for any excuse to take me there. Once I threw up three times in two days, so they took me to the vet. Another time they found a little bump on my head. Back to the vet. One day they saw me rubbing my eye. Away we went again. Sometimes I'm perfect and they still take me.

When they carry me in the front door of the office, I start to complain on general principles. The receptionist around the corner always says, "That sounds like Genevieve." You're darned right it's Genevieve, and you'd better believe that I'm not here to win friends and influence people!

Then I suffer the first humiliation. The receptionist picks me up and puts me on a scale right there in the lobby, where everyone can see. And she always repeats my weight out loud so everyone can hear. Listen—a lady's weight is private business. So what if I've gained a half-pound since I was here last? I had to go to a lot of holiday parties; I'll get back down after the New Year. How would she like it if I tripped her onto the scale and Denny called out her weight?

Then we have to go and twiddle our paws in the waiting room. And can you believe that I have to sit in there with, not only other dogs, but also cats and rabbits and birds? Why don't they have a separate (but equal) waiting room for nondogs, so I don't have to look at them and get more upset than I already am? And another thing—how could someone possibly look at a cat and conclude that something in particular was wrong with it? Everything about it is wrong from the beginning, but there's nothing that the vet can do about it.

I hate the music that they play. It's the same song every time I go there; it sounds like a slug dying on the piano keys. I think it's meant to calm us down, but it makes me want to fly through the ceiling. Why don't they play something by Three Dog Night or Snoop Doggy Dogg?

Another thing that bugs me is that all the magazines are so old. I like to look at the pictures while Denny or Katrina is reading, but I've seen the same pages so many times that I have them memorized. And somebody seems to have cut out all the pictures of cute male dogs.

Finally the nurse comes to get me. Katrina always goes in with me, but Denny stays outside. He says that it makes him too nervous. Can you imagine that? I'm the one that's going to get poked and prodded, and it makes *him* too nervous. Male humans are wimps.

The nurse leads us into a little room and puts me on a cold metal table. I hate that table. Then the vet comes in. She always kisses and hugs me, but I know it's just a trick to get my mind off what's to come. And I never do know what's to come. Sometimes she puts burny stuff in my eyes. Sometimes she jabs me with hurt sticks. Sometimes she puts something cold up my hiney. One time she blew something up my nose, and that really scared me because only a few nights earlier I had watched the movie *Scarface* with Denny and Katrina. And the whole time that the vet is torturing me, Katrina is telling me, "It's all right, Genevieve, it's all right." Well, if this is what "all right" feels like, I'll take a pass and let you get up on this table. All right?

Eventually the vet gets tired and lets Katrina pick me up. We go back to the front desk where the receptionist tries to make over me again, but all I want to do is get back out that front door into the fresh air. Katrina gives her a plastic thing out of her wallet, and then the receptionist gives it right back. I don't know what that's all about, but at least Katrina is not giving her any money, because I can hurt myself for free. I don't need to come here to do it.

At long last, Katrina takes me outside and we try to find Denny. He's usually hiding under a tree, where the vet can't find him. I can't get to the car fast enough, because I'm not going to be happy with life until I see this Chamber of Horrors getting smaller out the back window.

People have it easy; they never have to go to the vet. Except for Denny—he got treated by one once. Maybe that's why he hides under the tree now. The story goes back many years to when Denny's dog, Sardo, developed a problem with his paws. He had been licking his feet quite a bit, and then one day he just refused to get up from behind his chair. He wouldn't go for a walk and he wouldn't get up for a treat. At first Denny and his family feared that Sardo had suffered a stroke. But he seemed completely alert and not sick in any way. He just wouldn't stand up. When he started licking his paws again, Denny took a closer look and saw that his pads were badly infected, red and cracked and oozing. It was no wonder Sardo didn't want to move.

He had to be taken to the vet immediately, but everyone dreaded it because of what that did to him. And them. As a puppy, Sardo had decided on his very first visit to a vet that staying away from such a place was a cause worth fighting for. From then on, whenever he had to be taken back, he needed to be tranquilized and then manhandled into the building. Sardo was a guy I could have loved.

This time, Denny and his family decided to take Sardo to a new vet, in the hope that Sardo wouldn't realize what was happening until it was too late to do anything about it. They gave him a tranquilizer and then carried him to the car. It was decided that Denny would go alone, to keep the whole affair as low-key and casual as possible. (Denny had gotten his driver's license only a few months earlier, and this actually marked the first time that his driving had anything other than a recreational purpose.)

The vet's office was in an area of the countryside that Sardo had never visited before. Denny parked the car and then, leaning down and grasping Sardo's collar, led him up the walk toward the office. Sardo was following slowly, but willingly, and he didn't seem to notice the vet's sign. So far so good. There were no smells coming from the office (at least Denny didn't smell any) and no sounds (at least Denny didn't hear any).

As they approached the building, Denny looked up momentarily to see where he was going. He heard a snarl and looked down at what only an instant before had been a normal hand. It was now remainder bin material, bleeding from several scratches and lacerations along the fingers. Sardo ran back to the car and, finding it closed up, jumped through the open window of another car that was parked nearby. Maybe he had seen the vet's sign after all?

Denny went back down and found Sardo trembling and cowering in the back seat of the stranger's car, with the stranger trembling and cowering in the front seat. After a hurried explanation and apology to the wide-eyed stranger, Denny managed to get Sardo back into his own car, locked him safely away, and went up to the office to tell the vet what had happened.

Clutching bloody tissues around his injured hand, Denny entered a waiting room filled with people and their pets. The receptionist took one look and quickly ushered him into an examining room. No doubt the waiting clients were wondering why a human got such priority at the vet's.

The vet came in and cleaned the wounds, applied an antiseptic, and put a bandage on. He also advised Denny to get a tetanus shot, just to be safe. As Denny reemerged into the waiting room, he proudly held up his bandaged hand and exclaimed, "This guy is so good I think I'll bring my dog to him." Nobody laughed. Denny suspected that they were beginning to think that they had wandered into some kind of loony bin.

The vet and his assistant followed Denny to the parking lot to see if they could get Sardo up to the office, or at least have a look at his paws. As soon as they opened the car door, they were faced with more viciousness than they were prepared to deal with. They claimed never to have seen a family pet that wild in their lives. They also found it hard to believe that the dog actually lived in a house with people, all of whom were still alive.

They instructed Denny to take Sardo home, give him a much larger dose of tranquilizer, and then bring him back. This worked, and Denny's mom took a very sleepy and cooperative Sardo back to the vet for treatment, while Denny went to the emergency room for his own treatment—the tetanus shot. Sardo returned a few hours later, still under the effects of the tranquilizer and with all four paws bandaged. He promptly went to sleep in the bedroom.

Later that evening, they were all startled by a very authoritative knock on the door. Denny peered through the window to see two very stern-looking police officers. They had come to investigate a report of a vicious dog. The hospital, as required by law, had called the police station and reported the dog bite.

Denny was terrified that the officers were going to have Sardo taken away to Death Row, without benefit of a trial. Denny explained that he had been accidentally "nipped a little" by the family dog, who was in great pain and not thinking clearly. He told them how Sardo was normally the gentlest dog in the world, who wouldn't hurt a fly (except when he managed to catch one, but Denny didn't mention that). Denny felt like a married person trying to cover up for an abusive spouse after a domestic dispute.

Denny seemed to be doing a good job, because the officers started telling him that they wouldn't do anything to Sardo under the circumstances, but that it would be a different story if Sardo were to bite a stranger.

Just then, Denny heard Sardo growl weakly from his sickbed in the next room. "The tranquilizers must be wearing off!" he thought. He had this terrible vision of Sardo careening around the corner, his bandaged paws a blur, launching himself teethfirst at these boot-wearing, stick-carrying, blue-uniformed intruders.

"Oh, no, Sard! Please, don't do it!" Denny silently screamed.

The officers left unharmed. Denny leaned against the door in relief and realized that he was sweating from the tension. He walked to the next room to see Sardo, who was lying on a blanket. He wagged his tail when he saw Denny, but he made no effort to get up. Clearly, his paws were still hurting badly. That must have been the reason why he stayed out of sight of those policemen. Or was it?

Within a few days, Sardo had recovered nicely from his ordeal and, rehabilitated, resumed his role as a law-abiding citizen. Denny's hand healed up well, with only a few faint scars left as souvenirs. And in case you're wondering, the vet didn't charge Denny for his office visit. (Sardo was charged for his, though.)

11

Getting Skeeter

Go get Skeeter!"

Oh, no, here we go again. Want to know something? I don't want to go get Skeeter right now. I just want to lie here and daydream about my boyfriend, Barli. In fact, I rarely want to go get Skeeter. You see, Skeeter is a little, green froggy toy that Denny and Katrina bought me.

"Genevieve," they said, "This is Skeeter. Go get Skeeter."

And then they threw this Skeeter character into the corner. Well, you know me, if I see something new go flying across my living room and land in the corner, I'm darned sure going to get up and take a closer look at it. So I jumped up and got Skeeter. I have to admit, Skeeter was fun to play with for a few days. He even squealed when I bit him real hard. I loved that.

And just like clockwork, every few hours Katrina or Denny would start yelling, "Genevieve, where's Skeeter?"

This in spite of the fact that Skeeter was lying right there in plain sight, and certainly they *had* to be able to see him, too. Then I'd get a little worried that maybe they were going blind, so I'd hoist myself off my soft, warm cushion and go get Skeeter. They'd get all excited and tell me "Good Dog," and I'd know that their eyesight was just as good as ever. I don't know why I worry about them so much.

Well, this has gone on far too long now. And it's not just Skeeter. No, sir. At any given moment, I might be asked to go get Lambert, Honey, Baxter, the pork chop, the hanky, the sock, the disko, the puff, the puffbone, the buddabone, the basketball, Benjamin, Humpty, Charley, Santa, the twist, Morty, or, of course, Kong, their all-time favorite. I am really surprised that these humans can remember all those names, because in general they're not that sharp.

I'll give you an example. Why are Denny and Katrina so impressed when we're out driving in the car and I start getting excited ten miles before we get to our destination? Can't they smell where they're going, too? Honestly, sometimes I just want to bury my head in my paws when they get lost and have to look at their map, when I could find my way back home blindfolded.

I keep on having this dream (they think I'm chasing rabbits). In the dream, I wake up one morning and I can talk like humans. And then do I have some fun!

"Where's the *TV Guide*? Go get the *TV Guide*," I yell to them.

"Where's the telephone? Go get that phone!"

"I want the car key. Go find that key!"

And then I sit there on the couch and watch them go

scampering off to fetch all this junk, and when they bring it to me I just fling it right back across the room and make them go chase it again. I swear, when I have that dream I get so excited that my little legs start moving all around and I start breathing real funny.

Then the dream ends and someone is shaking me and yelling, "Genevieve, are you all right? Go get Skeeter."

Talk about waking up on the wrong side of the bed—that'll do it every time.

Well, you'll have to excuse me now. I've got to go get Skeeter.

Boy, I sure hope their eyes are OK.

12

The History of Dogs and People

By now, it should be clear that I'm divulging some doggy secrets that humans were never supposed to know. Many of my colleagues may get mad at me for this, but I have good reasons for doing it. First, people wouldn't read my book if it just contained the same information they could learn from their own pets. Hey, dirt sells! I'm giving you what you can't get at home. Second, if people had a better understanding of their dogs, they would give us pizza more often.

A much-studied topic among anthropologists is the history of the relationship between dogs and people. Like us, these scientists spend a lot of their time digging for bones. But, amazingly, when they find some, instead of chewing on them they clean them up and put them in museums. I've seen photos of mastodon displays and all I can say is "what a waste"—that's a weeklong dinner party for me and all my friends.

Scientists love to argue about things. They do this via competing theories. A scientific theory is supposed to explain how an event happened, and also predict such events in the future. I need to give you an example, so maybe you'll understand better.

One afternoon I barked at a squirrel, and an instant after that a big branch from a pine tree in the backyard fell down. Since this couldn't have been a mere coincidence, I formed a theory that the sound energy from my bark went out and banged against the branch and knocked it down. That was a smart theory because it explained why the branch fell down, and it also meant that I was one powerful puppy.

But now I had to test the theory by seeing if I could use it to predict more branches falling down. So the next day I stood in the backyard again and barked as loud as I could. (I stayed close to the house so that I wouldn't get hit by falling debris.) Absolutely nothing happened. This was hard for me to take because it meant that my theory was wrong. I was depressed for the rest of the day. But that evening, Katrina and Denny were watching the news, and it was showing a video of a tornado that had struck a town in Kansas that afternoon and blown down, not only trees, but also houses. And I realized that my theory had been proven correct after all. I just had to add another part to the theory to the effect that my bark gets stronger the farther it travels. That's why in science you have to be very careful before you jump to conclusions.

Scientists have jumped to many conclusions about the history of the relationship between dogs and people. Let me tell you what really happened.

My ancestors had it made in prehistoric times. All dogs looked exactly the same: shorthaired, rangy, brown, with small pointed ears. We liked it that way because it made dog shows impossible. We lived in perfect harmony with one other. We had good dog names like Gorg and Vard—there were no Fifis or Blackies or Creampuffs. The weather was warm and everything was lush and green. (There was a brief period of time when the giant refrigerator in the north went screwy and sent ice pouring down over the whole landscape. That was a real treat, because it was the first time we dogs got to chew on ice cubes.)

There were plenty of small creatures crawling around to eat, and the big reptile things were too slow and stupid to catch us. We actually watched them go extinct. What happened there was that they had this dino-seer who could look into the future. When he started telling them about the movie *Jurassic Park*, they all got so depressed they killed themselves. We ate real good for a while after that. That's why dogs love chicken so much today, because it tastes like dinosaur.

Then something new appeared on the scene: weird, hairy creatures that sometimes walked on their hind legs and sometimes on all fours. Dogs have argued ever since about where the first of these creatures came from, but the most prevalent view holds that it was New Jersey.

At first it was fun to watch these buffoons. We'd sit up on the rocks with a snack and watch the bison run over them. When they did manage to kill something, they'd start grunting and bumping their chests and high-fouring each other. The females climbed onto one another's shoulders and did flips and screamed encouragement through hollowed-out branches.

As time went on, they started lurking near our camps at night. Sometimes we'd wake up and see them crawling around, picking up our meat scraps. We'd bark and chase them away, but we didn't bite them because we were afraid it would make us sick.

After a few thousand years, we eventually got used to having them around. Initially we called the creatures "hermans," but over time the word got changed to "humans." We taught them how to play games with us, like fetch and hide-and-seek. We found that they could keep playing the same game over and over without getting bored. This was probably because their brains were so tiny in relation to their size. We also noticed that they liked to keep score, while we dogs enjoyed playing just for the fun of it. On one occasion, two of the humans ended up with exactly the same score, and one got so mad that he bashed the other over the head with a rock. That was the first "sudden death" overtime in sports.

Because of their flexible fingers, the humans were very good at tedious detail work. They started to make us little necklaces out of shells, and pillows out of straw. As a reward, we decided to teach them how to start a fire by striking rocks together. We had known how to do this forever, but it was tough on our paws. The humans were good at making fire, even though they seemed to think that it was great fun to throw it at one another. Now we had a nice warm campfire and pillows to lounge on every night. The humans were really coming in handy.

Soon the humans started making clothes for themselves out of animal skins. One of the more ambitious ones actually came out with a line of clothing made especially for hunting, with a little signature club embroidered on it. The humans all stood upright now, and some even snapped their fingers as they walked. They began to build shelters to live in, instead of caves. And then the first developer showed up and created Paleolithic Pines. It was built right alongside one of the major human migration paths, and there was a huge billboard that read, IF YOU LIVED HERE, YOU'D BE HOME BY NOW.

And that's when the trouble began. They started to take us to live with them in these shelters. That was no life for a dog. We couldn't hunt with our friends like we used to, we couldn't poop and pee inside the shelters because it would stain the straw, and they fed us food they wouldn't eat themselves. They even started to make rules, such as dogs had to have ropes attached to them in order to walk them outside. But worst of all, they started trying to tell us what to do. "Sit," "stay," "wait," "come," "heel"—of course, their language then was just a series of hisses and clicking sounds. That's the origin of clicker training.

We were in crisis. So in 20,000 B.L. (Before Lassie), we held a big convention in Las Vegas to plot our future. In a very close vote, it was decided that from then on we would pretend that humans were our superiors and masters. What we were getting in return for this ruse were free toys and the freedom to sleep twenty-three hours a day. The minority did manage to get a rider attached to the resolution: All future dogs were obligated to pay tribute to their proud heritage by occasionally showing utter contempt for their human masters. It was considered especially fitting if this were done during obedience training or dog shows.

And that's all I'm going to say on the topic. If anyone should ever ask you about it, remember—Genevieve didn't tell you nothing!

13

Chased, by Georges

Katrina hates storms. Having grown up in central Alabama, she has spent more than her fair share of time hunkered down in the cellar with her family, all the while hoping that the roaring noise from above didn't mean that the cellar had become the attic. As a result of these childhood experiences, any wind strong enough to mess up her hair is sufficient to get her camped out in front of the Weather Channel. Of all the places Katrina could have settled in with Denny, the last should have been a "velocity zone" on the west coast of Florida. I'm not exactly sure what a velocity zone is, but I think it refers to how fast your house would disappear if a hurricane were to hit the area.

On the other hand, Denny doesn't believe anything until he sees it. Years ago he began the six-hour drive from Albany to Boston, on his way to an interview. It was a beautiful winter day, bright blue sky and blinding sunshine.

He congratulated himself on having eluded his own personal curse, which in the past had always mandated that whenever he had to drive a long distance, he would find himself in the middle of a one-hundred-year weather event.

He had gone about halfway when he tuned into a popular radio station from Boston. But they weren't playing music. They were announcing all the closings and emergency measures being taken to try to deal with the monstrous, surprise snowstorm that had ambushed the city. All public transit had shut down, and thousands of commuters were trapped downtown.

Denny heard this, but he did not believe it. He was only a few hours from Boston and there wasn't a cloud in the sky. He thought momentarily about turning around and heading for home, but that seemed spineless. What was he going to trust, his own eyes or some stupid radio broadcast that could just as well be a joke? He kept driving. The emergency bulletin announcer kept talking.

An hour later, Denny left one world and entered another. The world he left was one where you could see the hood of your car. His new world was one in which a chaotic white curtain battered the windshield, where the car was sliding around like a drunken ice-skater, and the roar of the wind almost drowned out the semi-hysterical radio announcer.

Being an experienced winter driver, Denny instantly took action by beating his fists against the steering wheel and screaming obscenities in every mathematically possible combination. It took him more than an hour to exit the turnpike and reenter in the opposite direction, over sixty minutes of desperate maneuvering to escape a scary, brutal, icy nightmare. Hell had indeed frozen over.

But Denny was satisfied. He had seen the blizzard—now he believed it!

Needless to say, Katrina's and Denny's philosophies about when to evacuate because of an approaching hurricane differ slightly. During hurricane season, Katrina starts to pack whenever a cloud appears off the coast of Africa. And a cloud did appear there in September of 1998. Katrina announced to Denny that she had a bad feeling about it, and that he should start making plans. Denny said he already had a plan: "When I see a hurricane, we're going to get the hell out of here." Katrina was not impressed by Denny's emergency preparations.

Tracking the path of that cloud as it meandered slowly across the Atlantic became Katrina's main interest in life. She thought it was obvious that the cloud was in the process of blossoming into a Category 5 hurricane (the worst), and that its path clearly would take it due west across the ocean, around the southern tip of Florida, north for a few hundred miles, and then a sudden jog east for a direct hit on Sarasota. She would periodically yell for Denny to come look at the weather map, to see that she was right. Denny wondered to himself why the U.S. government spent so much money on meteorologists, computer networks, weather satellites, and reconnaissance planes, when Katrina could just stare at the weather map and issue much more accurate and timely forecasts.

Over the next few days, the little cloud got bigger and became a tropical depression. Katrina went out and bought duct tape for our windows, and tarps to cover the furniture. Then the depression started showing the hint of an eye. Katrina went to the supermarket and bought enough water to fill an Olympic-sized swimming pool, and half a ton of canned goods. A few days later, Katrina woke Denny up at six in the morning.

"You've got to come and see this."

Denny stumbled into the living room, where the Weather Channel was blaring. On the weather map was a gigantic white pinwheel that covered half the Atlantic Ocean. He was looking at Hurricane Georges.

"Well, do you believe me now?" asked Katrina.

"Look, just because it's a hurricane doesn't mean we're in any danger yet. It's still thousands of miles away. They don't even know yet if it's going to hit the U.S. mainland at all."

Katrina looked at Denny in a way that suggested that he might be dumber than a stump. She left for work, instructing him to keep the Weather Channel on at all times and to call her with any news. As soon as the garage door slammed shut, he turned off the TV and fired up the stereo. What could be more boring than to watch a hurricane crawling across a weather map at five miles per hour?

Several days later the hurricane had wheeled into the Caribbean and was tearing up the islands there. And then it started bending north, toward the west coast of Florida. Denny came home one afternoon to find Katrina sitting transfixed in front of the TV weather map. There was the faint outline of tiny, little Florida, and two inches away sat the white monster.

"How can you say that it's not going to hit us?" asked Katrina. "It's almost right on top of us now."

"Katrina, it's an optical illusion. Because of the size of the TV screen, everything is scrunched together. It's totally out of scale. It only looks like it's close to us. In reality, it's a very small thing in a very big expanse of water. It still can go anywhere. The chances of it hitting us are very small. Stop worrying!"

The next morning Katrina woke Denny up at 5:30. He was starting to get used to it. He staggered into the living room and slouched into the chair. The Weather Channel was on.

"Now what do you think?" asked Katrina, her manner eerily calm.

Denny stared at the map for a few minutes. He listened to the announcers. He looked over at Katrina.

"I think that miserable bastard is going to blow us away."

He went over to the telephone and started calling the major hotel chains, in the hopes of finding a vacancy somewhere in central Florida. This was not an original idea—several million other Floridians were doing exactly the same thing at that moment. It began to look as though they might have to drive as far as Georgia to find a room. Then he got lucky: there was one vacancy in Lakeland, about sixty miles inland. He made the reservation. Then he started packing. And taping up the windows. And storing valuables and important documents as high off the floor as possible. And tying tarps over the furniture.

In short, all the things Katrina had been telling him to do for a week.

"Where are we going to go?" asked Katrina.

"We got lucky. I found something in Lakeland."

"Lakeland? But that's in Polk County." She looked horrified.

"OK, what's wrong with Polk County?"

"It's the tornado capital of Florida. Anytime there's bad weather, they have tornadoes in Polk County."

"Katrina, listen. There's a big hurricane headed right for us. It could kill people. That's something we know. We've got to get out of here. The only room I could find in the whole state is in Lakeland. The chances of us getting hit by a tornado, even in Polk County, are almost nil. So it's just common sense that we go to Lakeland. And that's where we're going."

They took one last look around the house, to make sure they had done all they could do, and to fix the picture in their mind, in case they wouldn't see it again. Our car, packed tight with every household good you could imagine, looked like Okies heading for California. But I was excited: we were going on an adventure!

It had already started to rain as we headed north on I-75, before turning east toward Lakeland. Katrina kept scanning the sky, as if she were in training for the Civil Air Patrol. As soon as we crossed the Polk County line, the clouds started taking on colors you would never find in a crayon box. The wind blew harder and the rain pounded on the car; lightning flashed like a disco strobe and the thunder was punching out a very creative bass line. I got nervous and jumped into Katrina's lap. She was already nervous and was staring at Denny.

"I told you," she said.

"Well, what do you want to do? Do you want to drive to Georgia now, in this?"

Katrina didn't say anything, but I think that she did.

We arrived in Lakeland in the pouring rain, and pulled into the parking lot of the first restaurant we saw. In the rush that morning, no one had eaten a thing. I had my lunch in the car, and then Katrina put me into my softsider carrying case and we dashed into the restaurant. It was deserted. The hostess seated us in the corner, next to a big, rattling, plate glass window, and left menus. A few minutes later a man came over and introduced himself as the manager.

"Do you have a dog in that crate?" he asked.

"Yes."

"I'm sorry, but I'll have to ask you to either put it in your car, or else you'll have to leave. It's against the health code to bring a live animal in here."

I could tell by Denny's voice that his fuse had been lit. "OK, if we brought a dead one in, would that be all right?"

The manager seemed genuinely confused by the question. In fact, he looked the type to be confused by any question.

"Listen, we had to evacuate from Sarasota. We don't have much choice about our dog. She's enclosed in that crate and can't do any harm. You don't think you can make an exception under these circumstances?"

"No, I'm sorry."

Katrina picked me up and said, "Let's get out of this place." I could see Denny standing there, staring at the goofball. Then Denny followed us out. I was disappointed, because I wanted to see some action. We drove to another restaurant and had no problems there. They had great food. I know this because Katrina shared part of her lunch with me, handing me little bites through my partially open trap door.

We found our hotel and Denny went in to register. The parking lot was filled with cars from the coastal counties in the path of the hurricane. Denny came out and said, "They have a sign over the front desk that says that pets aren't allowed. I didn't say anything. We'll just have to hope for the best."

Denny parked the car and unloaded the suitcases; Katrina's, as usual, were as heavy as dwarf stars. Katrina draped my crate over her shoulder to make it look like luggage, and covered it with a towel. Then we went inside and found our room. I love new rooms. I ran all over, making sure everything smelled kosher.

Katrina headed straight for the TV and found the Weather Channel.

" . . . several tornadoes spotted in Polk County."

She looked at Denny and he started laughing. Then she started to laugh, too. I guess she finally decided that if she had to live with such a bonehead, she might as well try to find some humor in it.

It got dark and eventually Katrina and Denny settled in for the night. But I didn't want to go to sleep, because I was hearing noises out in the hall. Actually, I had been hearing noises in the hall the whole day, but they didn't start to bug me until Katrina and Denny went to sleep. I started barking to let the whole world know I was on duty.

Katrina and Denny got frantic and tried to hush me up. They told me that if I didn't stop barking, we could get kicked out of the room for hiding a pet.

I barked again. What was I supposed to do?

Then another dog started barking in the room to our left, and I had to yell at him, and then a dog totally lost his composure in the room to our right. We had just gotten into some good harmony when Katrina grabbed me and took me into the bathroom, shut the door, and turned on this noisy fan that sounded like a rocket ship taking off. I didn't want to compete with that, so I shut up.

When Katrina saw that I had become a sweet dog again, she carried me back out. But she left the fan going and she turned on the radio. Then she shoved me down under a pile of sheets and blankets, and told me to go night-night. I went right to sleep. But Denny and Katrina didn't get a moment's rest the entire night, because of the unholy racket from the fan and the radio. At least we didn't get kicked out.

At daybreak Katrina turned on the TV to see if we still had a home back home. Yes, we did. The storm had stayed out in the Gulf and missed Sarasota by about 150 miles. Sarasota had barely gotten any rain at all, while in Lake-land we were still getting drenched, listening to tornado warnings and watching small palm trees flying around the landscape. As it turned out, the people in Polk County would have been better off fleeing to Sarasota.

We drove home in the rain, which stopped almost as soon as we entered Sarasota County. Denny and Katrina spent the rest of the afternoon getting the house back into a livable condition. Denny found that when he removed the tape from the windows, it left a sticky mess that defied all known laws of nature. He scrubbed a small section of window for twenty minutes and managed only to move the blob from one place to another.

"Katrina, I'm telling you now, from now on I'm not going anywhere until I see our roof start to lift up."

But Katrina wasn't listening to him. She was watching the Weather Channel. There was a little cloud forming off the coast of Africa.

14

Party Animal

I didn't know what a party was; I'd never even heard the word before. So I didn't think anything was out of the ordinary when Katrina gave me a bath and brushed me and made me look even prettier than usual. But when she put a red velvet scrunchy with bells on it around my neck, I knew something good was in store. Katrina only puts scrunchies on me when we're going someplace special, like visiting friends.

We all got in the car and I watched closely where Denny was driving, just to make sure it wasn't to the vet. I don't have to tell you that the vet definitely doesn't count as some-place special, but maybe Katrina had gotten devious and dressed me up to throw me off the scent. But when Denny turned north I knew I was safe, because in order to get to the torture chamber you have to drive south.

Denny drove us to an area of town where one of my favorite places is located: Dinger's Dog Bakery. They sell all kinds of doggy cookies and treats there, and you can look into the glass cases and bark at what you want. The owners have told us that one of their most popular items is the mailman cookie, for obvious reasons. They also have doggy clothes and books. Whenever I'm there, after I pick out my treats I like to browse around and check out the latest word in canine fashion. No question about it——those clothes are made for putting on the dog.

We parked the car and I rocketed toward Dinger's, dragging Katrina behind me because she was walking too slowly. We got to the store and I couldn't believe it—a big sign in the front window said, "This is it! Happy First Birthday, Genevieve!" Was the sign for me? What's a birthday?

As we entered, someone yelled, "There's the birthday girl," and everyone started cheering and clapping. Hey, I must be the birthday girl, whatever that is. But I think I'm beginning to like it.

What I really wanted to do right then was pick out all my treats, but instead Katrina started pulling me to the back of the store. Why was she doing that? It was boring back there and I didn't want to go. I planted my paws and just flat refused to cooperate. Don't tell me you brought me all the way down here and now you're not going to let me buy stuff. I hadn't bitten a mailman in weeks.

Katrina, not wanting to mop the floor with my butt, picked me up and carried me to the back and then out a door. I had to blink twice at what I saw. The enclosed patio was decorated with ribbons and banners and balloons, and it was filled with people and dogs. Everyone was yelling, "Surprise, Genevieve. Happy birthday," and all the dogs were barking at me, too. And look who was there! My mommy, Chloe, and Sharon, and my half-sisters, Cecily and Emma. And there was my daddy, Calvin, and his owner, Arianne. And there were several puppies that looked a lot like me (they turned out to be my brothers and sisters from other litters; unfortunately, Heidi and Hunter had moved too far away and weren't able to come), as well as people I didn't even know. I couldn't wait to get down and greet all my guests. I loved parties!

I ran around licking everyone hello, even Calvin. I think he was happy to see me, but he seemed more interested in hitting on some of the other female dogs that were there, especially Chloe. He couldn't give it a rest even for my party, the old coot. He'll never change. I don't know why Chloe gives him the time of day. I know my boyfriend, Barli, wouldn't run around on me like that.

The humans were having just as much fun as we were, getting to know one another and exchanging stories. They kept telling Denny and Katrina that it was a marvelous idea to have a birthday party for me. I thought so, too. I'd better have another one real soon.

Denny had hired a nice man to take videos of my party, and when Curtis said that he had a dog, too, Denny invited Curtis to bring him along. The dog was named Lucky. Once I heard a joke about a dog that was deaf, blind, three-legged, and answered to the name of Lucky. Well, it couldn't have been the same dog because the Lucky at my party was only blind. He was sitting by himself near Curtis, and I felt sorry for him, so I went over to kiss him. I guess he couldn't see how pretty I was because he started growling at me and scared me. Chloe jumped right off Sharon's lap and rushed over to us. She licked me to make sure I was OK, and then she gave Lucky a scolding. It made me feel good to know that my mommy still loved me after all that time. Calvin, of course, paid no attention to any of it, because he was chasing a female around who was young enough to be his daughter (in fact, it was his daughter).

I had really worked up an appetite, so I was sure glad to see the "Dingerettes" bring out two birthday cakes. Time to pig out! But I got insulted when I found out that only one of the cakes was for us dogs—the spice cake with liver icing. Then they jammed a stick into my cake and started it on fire. Why were they burning my cake up before I had a chance to have any? Katrina picked me up and held me next to the cake so people could take pictures. I squirmed around, hoping that Katrina would drop me into the cake.

Then everyone started singing a song. I think they were singing the song to me, but I wasn't paying much attention to it because I was too concerned about my cake. I do know one thing: it was the longest song I've ever heard in my life. That's one thing I will never understand about humans. They put food in front of themselves and then, instead of diving right into it, they do silly stuff like clink their glasses together and make speeches, or sing songs. You put food in front of a dog and you'd better just keep your mouth shut and back off.

They finally finished singing, and Katrina told me to make a wish. OK, put that inferno out and let me into that cake! It worked because Katrina blew the fire out, but as she did I saw a little drop of spit go flying onto the cake. I definitely had to remember where that landed so that I didn't eat that gross piece of cake. Katrina started cutting the cake, luckily from the good side. She put a piece on a paper plate and then put it down for me. Oh, boy, it was so delicious. I might need to have birthday cake for every meal now. Everyone was watching me, as if they weren't sure if I was going to like it or not. Give me another, bigger piece and I'll show you whether I like it or not.

All my doggy guests loved the cake, except for Calvin. He was too busy. So I went over and ate his, too. The humans started eating their own cake, but it couldn't have been any good without the liver icing. As long as they stayed away from my cake, I didn't care what they ate.

Someone said, "Let's open the gifts." Katrina sat me on her lap next to a pile of boxes that were all wrapped up so you couldn't see what was inside. She took the first one and peeled the paper off. Then she opened the box and took out a little sweater. She pulled it over my head and my paws, so I guess it was mine. I'd never worn clothes before. It felt nice and warm, but I was afraid that I looked a little too human in it. Everyone told me how pretty I looked, so I guess it was all right.

Another box contained a white teddy bear that I call Snowflake. Snowflake is bigger than I am, and I love to wrestle him and chew on his nose; I think he's going to look a lot better when I finally get that thing off. I also got some pig ears to chew on and a little framed photo of my brother Spock (Spock was from the litter after mine). Spock looks a lot like me, so I adore the photo. And I got an

Autograph Hound, a big, stuffed hound dog on which everyone wrote a birthday greeting.

After I opened all my presents, it was time for the games. The first one was bobbing for bones. One of the Dingerettes put a cookie bone in a bowl of water, and we were supposed to try to fish it out. I hated to see a good cookie go to waste like that. I tried to get hold of it with my teeth, but the water got into my nose and made me mad. Then I tried to kick the cookie out of the bowl, and everyone started laughing. After that I didn't want the soggy old thing anyway, so I just quit. Spock tried for a while, but he came up empty, too. My other guests decided that drowning was too high a price to pay for a wet cookie, so they refused to play.

Then the Dingerettes announced that it was time to play musical chairs. Each owner had to carry his dog during the game; we started with eight people and their dogs. Seven chairs were lined up, alternately facing front and back. When the music started playing, everyone had to march around the chairs until the music stopped. Then you had to sit down in one of the chairs. Try to work the math out for yourself here. Only humans could think of something so ridiculous.

But if they were going to make me play, I wanted to win. Unfortunately, Denny was my partner, so I knew that I didn't have much of a chance. You see, moving fast is not one of Denny's assets in life. The only time I've seen Denny react quickly was the night I found a snake in the living room. Denny was lying on the couch, watching TV. I saw the snake in the corner and I thought I should say something, so I started barking at it. Denny didn't pay any attention to me. He probably thought I was barking at something I heard outside. For some reason, Denny and Katrina don't seem to care about the world outside when they're in the house. My attitude is this: if it's living and isn't a plant, it doesn't belong within a half-mile of my yard.

I kept barking. Finally Denny said, "Genevieve, what is it?" He looked over the back of the couch at me. I looked at the snake and barked some more. Denny looked at the snake and flew up and over the couch like a singed Ninja. He ran and got a broom and a box, carefully managed to sweep the snake into the box, and threw the whole evil mess outside. Then he peeled Katrina off the ceiling. Just as soon as she was able to breathe and talk at the same time, she declared that she was moving back to Alabama immediately, unless Denny searched the whole house to make sure it had not become a serpentarium. Denny did this and found nothing more than several litters of dust bunnies.

But I had never seen Denny move like that again, so I didn't hold out much hope for winning at musical chairs. The music started and around and around we went. Every time we passed by an empty chair I got more nervous. Then Denny, in an unusual display of intelligence, grabbed a chair and tried to carry it around with us, but everyone started screaming at him so he put it back down.

The music stopped suddenly, there was a mad scramble, and the next thing I knew everybody was sitting down. Except us. I could not believe this. It was my party and because of Denny I was a big loser. They should have let us dogs play by ourselves. I started kicking for Denny to put me down. I didn't want to be near the dumb game any more; I wanted to get another piece of birthday cake. While I was over in the corner stuffing my face, someone won the game, but I couldn't tell you who it was because it didn't concern me.

Soon my guests started to leave, and everyone told me how much they had enjoyed my party. I was sad; I didn't want it to be over. All the dogs got a bag of Dinger's cookies to take home with them. Then we were the last ones left, and we said good-bye to the nice Dinger's people and drove home. I was so tired that I let Denny drive by himself. I curled up and took a birthday nap in his lap.

Several weeks later, we went back to Dinger's and I got so excited. I was having another party! But there was no birthday sign in the window—that worried me a bit. As soon as we got in the store, I ran to the back door and started scratching at it. I didn't want to miss a thing out there. But when Denny opened the door and I ran out, the patio was empty. No balloons or banners or people or dogs. To sum it up—no party. Then Denny explained to me that you only have a birthday party once a year. I should have known that humans would find a way to screw things up. Why couldn't I have a birthday party every week?

Katrina must have read my mind, because she was working on a Big Idea. I wasn't going to have to wait a whole year for my next party after all.

I'm the cute one—on the left.

Learning to guard my toys at an early age.

A dazed Denny holds me for the first time at Sharon's.

Katrina shows me around my new home. The jury is still out.

Centerfold

Barli and I practice for our wedding.

My first birthday party—Denny screwing up at musical chairs.

Do you think the sleeves are too short?

OK, I got Skeeter. Are you satisfied?

Hurricane Georges is coming? Get me out of here!

Put me in, Coach!

OK, it's a cathouse. So, sue me!

117

Teaching a lesson to a Christmas intruder.

Somebody turn off that danged alarm clock!

15

Playdays at the Paw Park

Without doubt, the all-time greatest achievement of human government can be found right here in Sarasota County. We have Paw Park, a large fenced-in area where we dogs can run free, while our humans sit in the shade and admire us. Since the county has a strict leash ordinance, I like to think of the park as an independent kingdom ruled by dogs, where we are beyond the reach of silly, human laws. We manage our own affairs, guided by a complex code of canine etiquette.

Paw Park had its grand opening a few months before my birthday party. Katrina let me pick out a scrunchy to wear and off we went. When I saw the park out of the car window for the first time, I absolutely lost it. Dogs were running and jumping all over a gigantic lawn, barking and yelping and having loads of fun. It was the cat's meow! And their humans seemed to be keeping their noses out of the dogs' business. I liked what I saw and I wanted to be in the middle of it. I started jumping against the dashboard, trying to make the car go faster. I haven't yet figured out which switch-thing Katrina and Denny push to make the car speed up, but as soon as I do our car rides are going to take a lot less time.

Katrina parked the car and then carried me in her arms over to the fence, where we had to go through a double gate to get inside. I was doing my best siren imitation to let everyone know that I had arrived, but I think I overdid it. A mob of dogs descended on us and scared poor Katrina silly; some of the dogs were as big as Katrina, so I guess that's understandable. They were all trying to check me out and flirt with me. I didn't mind; I may have a boy-friend, but I'm not dead.

Katrina headed for the nearest picnic table, leading a huge parade of my admirers. As soon as she sat down, still holding me, a dog as big as a rhino started sniffing my butt. I let that go for a few seconds, because it never hurts to be friendly. But it got to the point where I figured that he knew everything about me that he needed to know, and now he was getting a little too personal. So I lunged at him and snarled right in his oversized face. He was so shocked that he almost tripped over himself backing up, but my little virtue-saving display seemed to outrage all the dogs, and they started growling at one another—and at Katrina and me. Several humans rushed over and apologized as they grabbed their cattle-disguised-as-dogs and led them away. I yapped at them as they went, to let them know what was in store if they ever came back and bothered us again.

At that point, a very disappointed Katrina beat a retreat through the double gate, leaving several of my fans howling mournfully on the other side of the fence. As soon as she got home, she called her friend Ruth to describe what had happened. Ruth owns Filou, a male Yorkshire terrier that I use on occasion to make Barli jealous. Ruth told Katrina that she had had a similar experience at the park; a big dog had actually attacked Filou, and Ruth had been lucky to save Filou from major harm.

Ruth and Katrina had been looking forward to the opening of Paw Park for months, and now it looked as though their first visit was going to be their last. They both agreed that the park needed a separate section for small dogs. The question was, could the county be persuaded to spend more money just to accommodate economy-sized models like Filou and me?

Ruth and Katrina decided they would each call the county Parks and Recreation Department and make their plea. Katrina did so and was told that her suggestion was a terrific idea and that it would be brought before the staff. Ruth was told the same thing. But both Ruth and Katrina felt that some additional ammunition was needed. Filou was happy to oblige. He dictated the following letter to Ruth, which she promptly sent off to the Parks and Recreation Department:

December 4, 1998
Department of Parks & Recreation
Re: Dog Parks

To the Big Boss:

Hi, I'm Filou (that's French for Rascal). I'm a gorgeous Yorkshire terrier, weighing almost five pounds. I am eighteen months old. It is absolutely, definitely, positively high time for me to start socializing (how else am I supposed to meet that "special girl"?). So my two-legged mommy took me to the Paw Park on 17th Street. But guess what—my excitement turned into total frustration: she did not let me off the leash because all the big dogs running around there could hurt me.

For instance:

There are those Rotten 18-weiler trucks (their feet are as big as my head)

Then those bulky Bulldozers with the smashed-in noses (they roll over and crush everything)

The guys from Germany who lie about their job (they have never even seen a sheep)

The camouflaged, black-and-white spotted, Disney Characters

The clumsy, overstuffed, Golden Teddy Bears (I've never seen them bring anything back)

And worst of all, the speeding guys on stilts who dash by as if they have to catch the Orient Express (none of them is actually gray)

I'm telling you, it's a zoo out there! So, being so little (by stature, certainly not by heart or intelligence), I could end up mashed and looking like a leftover Yorkshire pudding! Of course, I feel left out, even discriminated against. Why can only big ones have fun? Little guys have rights, too!

Here is my request: separate a small section of the park for us miniature breeds (up to ten pounds). Because me and my tiny friends want to have fun, too.

Forever grateful,

Filou

P.S. And hurry up—I'm not getting any younger!

Filou's letter did it! Within days, he had an answer.

Sarasota County Government
Sarasota, Florida
Parks & Recreation Department

December 8, 1998

Dear Filou (Rascal):

In my thirty-six years as Director of the Parks &
Recreation Department, I have received hundreds
of letters from many folks, but never, ever an
adorable little dog. I was thrilled that you took
the time to express your feelings about Paw Park!

I immediately shared your letter with my staff
and will consider a separate section of Paw Park
just for miniature breeds like you and your tiny
friends. (We certainly wouldn't want Yorkshire
pudding on our hands.) When we have this
completed, we would like to have you and your
two-legged mom cut the ribbon to this new
addition to the park. We will contact you when
this project is completed.

Well, I've got to go chase my tail—Sarasota
County Government can be a dog-eat-dog world!

Your Pal,

Walt Rothenbach, Top Dog

A few months later, Filou and I attended the ribbon-
cutting ceremony for the small dog section, and we got to
meet all the dignitaries in attendance. I'm sure they hadn't
realized before what a strong lobby group we little dogs
are. Now they had to respect us and keep us happy, because we have long memories and there's always another
election coming up.

Now that we had our own section, we could romp and
play without fear of getting run over by the SUCs (sport

utility canines). In fact, one of our favorite games was to gather by the fence that separates the two sections and make fun of all the Goliaths. The big oafs would just sit there and look pitiful while we yapped away at them. Good fences make brave neighbors.

Katrina could finally begin to put her plan into action, the one she had been formulating ever since my birthday party. Her idea was to form a club, named Suncoast Social Butterflies, that would consist of area papillons (and other small breeds) and their humans. The club would meet every second Saturday afternoon at the park. It would be like having a party every couple of weeks.

In a year, the club has grown to over sixty dogs. I'm the president and I even have my own business cards. Recently, the city newspaper published a section on local nonprofit clubs and organizations, and we got a listing there. Shortly after, I got an invitation in the mail, addressed to me, to attend a community luncheon at the local Hyatt. I wanted to go so bad, but Denny and Katrina wouldn't let me. They said that the food wouldn't be healthy for me. But I think that the real reason was that they have no confidence in my table manners. They have only themselves to blame for that, since they insist on putting my dishes on the floor.

It would be different if I lived in France. Dogs there are rightly considered to be worthy dinner companions. In fact, a few years ago Katrina and Denny were dining in a fine restaurant in Paris, and they looked over to see a poodle seated at the next table. The poodle had a bib around his neck and was thoroughly enjoying the fine cuisine on his plate. Katrina and Denny thought this was wonderful. However, they were a bit afraid that the poodle, a Frenchman to the core, would light up a cigarette after the meal and blow smoke in their direction. Happily, he refrained.

We've had as many as seventeen papillons attend our Paw Park get-togethers. I've made a lot of new friends and, if Barli ever breaks my heart, I've got several suitors that are ready to step up to the plate. We've got quite a few different personality-types in our club. Some dogs stick close to their owners and don't socialize very much. A few go running around like maniacs as soon as they're let off the leash. Others get obsessed by another dog and then spend the entire afternoon making that dog's life miserable. Some hide under the benches and snap at anything that comes near them.

I guess we're not that different from humans after all.

16

Dear Genevieve

Because I'm a famous writer, other dogs assume I'm brilliant and know everything. Although this is not generally a reliable conclusion to draw, in my case they're absolutely right. So every week I get hundreds of letters from dogs around the world, asking me all kinds of questions. I try to answer as many as I can, but because of my busy schedule I can't respond to all of them. But this is a good opportunity to answer some of the more interesting letters. I have edited them for readability and to remove the compliments and marriage proposals that they usually contain.

Letter 1

Dear Genevieve,

In my house there is a little push-thing on the wall in each room, and when my humans touch it the room gets real dark or real bright. Since I'm a smart dog, I know that there has to be the same kind of push-thing outside, because sometimes it's real dark out and sometimes real bright. But I have never been able to find it. Do you know where it is?

Love,
Dancer

Dear Dancer,

I hate to tell you this, but you're wrong. Have you noticed that the light/dark cycle in your house is highly erratic, whereas outside it's a very regular and predictable pattern? This is over-whelming proof that there is no switch outside, or else it could get dark at noon and light at mid-night, and we all know it doesn't do that. Instead, I believe that the outside is on some sort of timer, like the kind humans use when they go away on vacation to make bad people think someone is home. I'm looking for this timer, and when I find it I'm going to reset it so that it gets dark for three hours each afternoon, during my naptime.

Kibbles and Kisses,
Genevieve

Letter 2

Dear Genevieve,

I want to be the first dog to run for political office. What do you think?

Love,
Chip

Dear Chip,

You're already a son of a bitch. Don't make it any worse.

Kibbles and Kisses,
Genevieve

Letter 3

Dear Genevieve,

How does television work?

Love,
Cossette

Dear Cossette,

Television is all based on computer chips, which are similar to potato chips, except that they don't taste good. When humans press the buttons on that little thing they hold in their hand, the computer chip creates miniature people, houses, cars, trees, dogs, etc., inside the TV, and then these tiny things go about their business just like the big ones do outside the TV. Because the computer chip makes up all these things, they don't have a scent like they're supposed to. The humans never know just what the computer chip is going to create, and that's why they're always pushing the buttons to make the chip change its mind. For some reason, humans are absolutely fascinated by these miniature worlds, whereas we dogs much prefer the real one.

Kibbles and Kisses,
Genevieve

Letter 4

Dear Genevieve,

How can we explain to our humans why we papillons get the zooms (where we go flying around and around the house at supersonic speeds)?

Love,
Dolly

Dear Dolly,

I would ask your humans to imagine how they would act if they just learned that they had won five billion dollars in the lottery. Well, we papillons often feel that way for no good reason at all. Aren't we lucky?

Kibbles and Kisses,
Genevieve

Letter 5

Yo, Genevieve,

I've heard that you will not touch your dry food until about two o'clock in the morning. Why is that?

Love,
Dickie-dog

Dear Dickie-dog,

I need to be ready to gulp down any REAL food that Katrina and Denny might offer me during the day. Dry food is not real food. You never see humans eating it, do you? (Sometimes Denny pretends to for my benefit, but his act is so bad that I just sit there and stare at him in amazement.) I've learned that by two o'clock in the morning all the good stuff has been put away, and so at that point I have nothing to lose. To paraphrase a song I heard on the radio the other day, the dry food all gets tastier at closing time.

Kibbles and Kisses,
Genevieve

Letter 6

Dear Genevieve,

Do you realize it's been over a month since you've been over to see me? You know how much the girls and I enjoy your visits. And you're two years old and you're not even thinking about making me a grandmother yet. Do you think you're going to be young and pretty forever?

Love,
Chloe

Dear Mom,

C'mon, Mom, you know I love you. It's just that Denny has had me working so hard on my book that I haven't had any free time at all. I promise I'll come by next week. And please stop nagging me about puppies. I'm a career-dog, Mom. I have other things I want to do with my life right now. I watched how you had to struggle to raise me and Heidi and Hunter all by yourself, while my daddy ran all over town chasing anything with four legs. I don't want that to happen to me. So just be patient, Mom. I'll make you proud of me, I promise.

Love,
Genevieve

Letter 7

Dear Miss Genevieve,

Have you ever been a bad dog and destroyed anything around the house?

Love,
Pearlie Mae

Dear Pearlie Mae,

Are you a reporter or something? I shouldn't have to answer a question like that. But to show you I've got nothing to hide, yes, I went through a period in my younger days when I chewed holes along the edges of the living room rug. I thought it made the rug look better, but Katrina and Denny didn't agree. I've learned from my mistakes, and now I never miss an opportunity to lecture young dogs about the evils of chewing on rugs.

Kibbles and Kisses,
Genevieve

Letter 8

Dear Genevieve,

My humans want to start me on agility training, but I hate regimented exercise. What should I do?

Love,
Spock

Dear Spock,

Take the agility training. It will get your humans into shape, and if you're lucky you'll see them fall on their butts.

Kibbles and Kisses,
Genevieve

Letter 9

Dear Genevieve,

What is the best way to make my humans feel guilty?

Love,
Boo

Dear Boo,

That's an easy one. The next time your people are going out and you realize that they're not taking you with them, act very excited and happy, run and bounce off the door, go fetch your leash and wag your tail until your whole body is shaking. This is about the worst thing you can do to your humans, and you will find it thoroughly enjoyable.

Kibbles and Kisses,
Genevieve

Letter 10

Dear Genevieve,

Which is your favorite toy?

Love,
Imbi

Dear Imbi,

My very first toy is still my favorite—the little basketball that Katrina had hidden away in her closet even before I was born. She loved me even then!

Kibbles and Kisses,
Genevieve

17

Agility Champion

People frequently ask if I'm going to go through agility training. Of course not. I don't need any training. I've got a course laid out right in my own house, and it's far tougher than the ones I've seen the competition dogs running around in. The thing is, there doesn't seem to be any purpose to what they're doing. They run and jump and weave for all they're worth, and then they get back to where they started and it's all over. Maybe they get a treat. Wow. When I do my agility work, on the other hand, there's a darned good reason for it.

The Blanket Tunnel

This is an absolutely essential move for any dog sleeping on a bed. Let's say you're having a nice snooze on top of the covers and you get a little chilly, or someone is trying to pet you, or the light is too bright. Get up and stick your nose underneath the blanket or sheet, and toss your head up with a quick, little jerk. Move under a few inches and do it again. Repeat this as often as necessary until you've found the perfect hideaway spot, then settle down and get back to business.

The Bed Vault

If your humans work to keep you living in style, they will generally get out of bed around sunrise. There is absolutely no need for you to get up this early. Let them fumble around the house and take a shower and get dressed and bump into things. You stay cozy and go back to sleep. But when you hear the refrigerator door opening and dishes banging around, you have no time to waste. It is imperative that you make your presence known in the kitchen immediately. Don't bother stretching or climbing down from the bed slowly. Take a flying leap and make sure you're already running when you hit the floor. If you're just a puppy, humans seem worried that you'll hurt your legs by doing this. In that case, I'd advise biting the bullet and getting up with your working humans. Let them pick you up off the bed without struggling. It's a bitch, I know, but remember that this is only temporary until you get a little older and can make your own schedule.

The Jack-in-the-Box

When you get into the kitchen, you'll see your humans preparing breakfast at the counter. Position yourself slightly to one side and a few inches behind them. Then leap at their legs and bang into them with all fours. The trick is to do this at least once per second for several minutes. It is important that as you impact their legs you give a little kick, as this adds invaluable emphasis. The higher up you can strike, the more effective it is. (There also seems to be a nerve in the back of the human knee which, when hit just right, causes the leg to buckle. Experiment with this at your own risk.) When you get really good at the Jack-in-the-box, you may want to throw in a few cabinet strikes. That is, at random intervals jump into the kitchen cabinet or appliance instead of your humans' legs. You can generate really neat sounds by banging against dishwashers and stoves. Keep jumping until your desperate humans give you some of their breakfast. Any attempt to give you dog food should be ignored.

The Human Pull

Before you go out for a walk with your human, make sure the leash is attached firmly to her hand. Once outside, this will enable you to drag her wherever you wish. If you let your human lead you, she will take you to boring places that have no meaning, like sidewalks and curbs. It is up to you to make the walk what you want it to be. If you want to go sniffing around under that bush, drag your human over to it. If your human resists, get real low and push with your back legs as hard as you can. Your front legs will tend to come up off the ground. Avoid this if possible, as it reduces your towing capacity. You may think you're too small to drag a human around. You are wrong. If you could see me yanking Denny and Katrina all over this green earth, you'd then realize what the proper application of five or ten pounds of power can do.

The Inclined Face

When your human falls asleep on the couch while watching TV, it presents one of the most challenging of all the agility events. Get a running start from at least ten feet away, leap, and land directly on his stomach. Your human will start to rise up in the struggle to regain the breath you've just knocked out of him. Before he's reached the full upright position, run right up his chest and over his face. Proper execution requires that all four paws impact the face at least once: Deduct a point for each paw that does not.

The Claw Windmill

This maneuver requires both endurance and balance. It should be employed only when your human is not listening to what you're saying. For example, I like to execute the claw windmill when Denny is trying to play his guitar. Rear up on your hind legs, extend the claws on your front paws, and pretend that you're digging for something very important two inches below the surface of your human's leg. Done correctly, this will leave a pretty pattern of welts and scratches, though if you draw blood you've gone too far. I guarantee that your human will drop whatever he's doing and pay attention to you.

The Zooms

Few things in life are as much fun as getting the zooms. You can get the zooms anywhere in the house, but I find the best place is the living room because of all the challenging obstacles. For a proper zoom, start running as fast as you can, pin your ears back, and drop your tail. You also want to assume a slightly scrunched-up posture to reduce wind drag. Go over couches, under chairs and tables, around lamps, all without breaking stride or reducing velocity. If you have to negotiate a tight turn next to a wall, I have found it helpful to actually run up onto the wall and use it like a banked track. Stop only when you feel nauseous or start wheezing. When should you get the zooms? This is entirely up to you. I like to get them when I've got too many tennis balls rolling around at once, or when I've stolen something and Denny or Katrina is chasing me, or when anyone teases me and says, "I'm gonna get you." A word of advice—don't get the zooms if you've got to go poopy.

The Crawl

When I want to veg out and not be bothered, I like to hide under the couch. But the space beneath it is only about three inches high, so I've got to make myself into a papillon pancake by getting flat on my belly and crawling. The only disadvantage to being under the couch is that if I hear someone go into the kitchen, it takes me several very valuable seconds to scramble back out. For this reason, I avoid performing the crawl around mealtimes.

The Barking Pushup

Your humans rely on you to warn them about noises outside the house. First of all, they do not hear well at all, and they can't point their ears like we can. But worse, even when they do hear a noise outside, they seem to take it for granted. "It's just the paperboy, or the garbage truck, or the wind." Well, we don't buy it. Any noise I hear outside, I'm assuming it's the ugliest, most humongous, flesh-eating space alien in the universe. And I'm going to bark until proven otherwise, or it blasts off and goes back to where it belongs. Threats like this demand the barking pushup. Throw your head back and explode with a screech. Your front paws should come off the ground several inches, and you should exhibit a well-formed pucker-butt. Continue this for at least an hour and a half, just to be sure. Even after the crisis is over, you should still bark or growl every few minutes to let the creep-thing know that you're still on the case. Your humans will be truly grateful, especially if you save them this way in the middle of the night.

18

Herd on the Street

When I'm out in the world, hordes of people ask Katrina and Denny the same questions about me, over and over. So, as a public service, I've decided to answer these questions here, once and for all.

Q: Is that a longhaired Chihuahua?

A: Are you kidding me? Can't you recognize a European aristocrat when you see one? Why those José-come-lately Chihuahuas weren't even identified until the late 1800s, while my relatives watched as Marie Antoinette became a head of her time. You'll find my image in all the great art museums of the world. Look for José and his cousins in TV commercials.

Q: Is she friendly?

A: No, I'm licking your shin because it tastes like chicken.

Q: Does she bark a lot?

A: I bark when it's called for. It's called for when I hear any noise that I didn't make. Or when I see any person or animal on the other side of a pane of glass. Or when someone is cooking something I like, and I just have to have some NOW. Or when I see any object in my neighborhood that wasn't there yesterday. Or when my ball rolls under the bureau, and I'd rather have someone else get it. Or when I watch nature programs on TV. Or when Denny or Katrina comes home. Other than that, I never bark.

Q: How old is she?

A: How old are you?

Q: Has she been fixed?

A: I wasn't broken!

Q: Are you going to breed her?

A: I'm too busy with my writing career to think about puppies anytime soon. I'm also afraid that getting pregnant will ruin my figure.

Q: Where does she sleep?

A: Between Denny and Katrina. This cuts down significantly on their mating activities, which is good, because I hate being left out of stuff.

Q: Is she smart?

A: Next question.

Q: Will you board her when you go on vacation?

A: No, no, no, no, no, no, no.

Q: Where do you keep her when you have to go out?

A: They put me in a big metal cage in the kitchen. Katrina refuses to refer to it as a "cage." She insists that it be called a "crate." I prefer not to quibble about definitions. It's a container with steel bars, and when I'm inside it I CAN'T GET OUT. Even worse, they turn the radio on to keep me company, and tune it to an easy-listening station. I will tell you this: the next time I have to listen to Helen Reddy singing "That Ain't No Way to Treat a Lady," I'm going to poop in my . . . crate.

Q: Are you planning to show her?

A: Show me what? They've already taught me all they know.

Q: Does she mind?

A: I certainly do, but I'll forgive you.

Q: Is she a happy dog?

A: I was until a few minutes ago.

Q: Will she get any bigger?

A: I'm six lean-and-mean pounds of muscle and fur, and I stand a good ten inches in my bare paws. Why would any dog want to get bigger than that?

19

Do Humans Think?

The question of whether or not human beings think has intrigued canine philosophers for thousands of years. For example, we have this from the writings of Fido the Elder, circa 576 B.S. (Before Snoopy):

"I question not that humans feel pain and have emotions that are somewhat akin to our own. Certainly, most all of us have at some point in our lives bitten a human and then experienced great guilt at having done so. Such guilt would have no logical basis if we did not assume that the unfortunate animal was experiencing pain of a type familiar to us. However, it is a far different and more difficult question as to whether humans have the capacity for thought. Those of us who live with humans are well aware that their behavior generally does not seem directed by any overriding self-consciousness or goal-oriented concepts. And yet, there are those times when we must stand back and regard with awe those actions of human beings that are so downright stupid that we cannot possibly attribute them to instinct or mere biological reactive mechanisms. Yes, my fellow canines, it is precisely at these times that we cannot help but conclude that these beings are blessed with a primitive form of thought."

In order to tackle this issue ourselves, we must first define what we mean by "thought." One hallmark of thought is self-consciousness, the awareness of self as an independent, self-directed entity within the larger environment. For example, we dogs do not have a great interest in looking at ourselves in mirrors. This is because we know that it is ourselves that we are regarding, and we know full well how we appear to others. Staring at ourselves in the mirror gives us no additional information, and we can better utilize our time by checking to see if anyone is sneaking a snack in the kitchen.

Humans, on the other hand, spend an inordinate amount of time looking at themselves in mirrors. When they get up in the morning, they study their image as if seeing something for the first time. They do it again before leaving the house. While driving they do it in those little mirrors stuck on the window of their cars. (Human females seem especially prone to this behavior. Because of this, I plan to make a fortune by inventing huge mirrors that will drop down from stoplights when they turn red, so that women won't have to yank on the mirrors in their cars and make their husbands mad.)

This human fascination with mirrors seems to indicate that they do not recognize their own images and have no sense of self. This, then, is evidence against human thought.

Another indicator of thought is the use of tools. For example, we use balls, blankets, pillows, and sticks to aid us in our daily endeavors. Here, humans score extremely high. Last week, Denny and Katrina took me into a store called Home Depot, and I couldn't believe all the tools humans have. In fact, unlike us, humans can't seem to do anything *without* tools. So, this evidence from tool use cuts both ways. The fact that humans use tools lends credence to human thought. On the other hand, their total dependence on tools could be taken as evidence that they don't have enough sense to do things the straightforward and natural way, like we do. Therefore, human use of tools is inconclusive with respect to the question of whether or not they think.

Communication via language is generally considered to be a certain sign of thought. Do humans exhibit language use? Certainly, the sounds they make are nothing like those we employ to communicate with one another. Denny and Katrina sometimes do make barking or whining sounds, but it's clear that they are merely parroting our language and have no understanding of the meanings. For example, the other day while Katrina was playing with me, she started barking in a way that sounded very much like, "If you don't get your mangy butt out of my yard right now, I'm going to take a big bite out of your hide." This was totally inconsistent with her playful behavior at the time.

Another example. Last night, Denny started whining and whimpering at me in a way that sounded like, "Please, please, let's go for a ride in the car and get some pizza."

But he couldn't have meant this, since he was lying on the couch holding his bloated belly after stuffing his face at dinner.

Do humans communicate with one another via those strange verbal sounds they make? Based on my observations, it's unlikely. First of all, when humans gather they all tend to make these sounds at the same time. They seem much more intent on making their own sounds than in listening to those made by other humans. This appears to be more a case of biological display than a process of communication.

Second, humans make these same sounds even when there are no other humans anywhere in the vicinity. For example, when Denny spills food all over himself in the kitchen, he jabbers quite loudly for minutes, even though Katrina is out and I'm busy tending to the overspray on the floor.

So, all things considered, the evidence seems to indicate that the sounds humans make do not constitute language.

Finally, what about the above passage by Fido the Elder, where he notes that the utterly foolish behavior of humans cannot be blamed on instinct or mere reaction, but must be taken as a sign of a rudimentary intelligence? This, to me, is the strongest argument available for attributing thought to our furless friends.

None of us can prove the issue one way or the other. Rather, I believe the prudent course is to assume that humans do think and to treat them with the dignity and respect we demand from one another.

So, cherish your humans and open your hearts to them. You'll find that their ability to accept and return love is unrivalled in the animal kingdom that we all share.

Appendix

How Intelligent is Your Human?

In the final chapter we concluded that, in spite of evidence that is less than overwhelming, it is best for us to assume that humans do think. This naturally leads to the next question: how intelligent are human beings? The issue of intelligence in humans is a fairly new field, since it is only in the last few years that dogs have come to believe it worthy of study. Based on my own extensive research conducted during almost two years of living with humans, I have developed a test that any of you can use at home to measure how smart your humans are.

Make sure your human is well fed and relaxed before beginning the test. Don't get frustrated or impatient with your human if he or she doesn't seem to be performing well. Keep in mind that no human does well on every part of the test. Treat it as a game and, above all, have fun.

Keep a tally of the points scored as you complete the various parts of the test. At the end of this appendix, you'll find a key to help you interpret your human's performance.

Good luck!

1. In the middle of the night, while your human is
   sleeping soundly, start barking hysterically.
   Your human:
   a) Continues sleeping.   0 points
   b) Tells you to keep quiet.   1 point
   c) Crawls under the bed.   2 points
   d) Gets on the floor and starts
      barking with you.   3 points

2. While your human has you out for a walk, pee on the
   tire of a car right in front of its owner.
   Your human:
   a) Yanks the leash and yells at you.   0 points
   b) Wipes the tire off with a tissue.   1 point
   c) Sniffs the tire.   2 points
   d) Pees on the tire, too.   3 points

3. The next time your human has a guest, jump on the
   visitor's leg and start humping.
   Your human:
   a) Orders you to get down.   0 points
   b) Pulls you off.   1 point
   c) Laughs.   2 points
   d) Starts humping the other leg.   3 points

4. Stand in front of the refrigerator and whine.
   Your human:
   a) Ignores you.   0 points
   b) Asks you what's wrong.   1 point

     c) Offers you a doggy snack.   2 points

     d) Gives you an entire chicken
        and a pizza.   3 points

5. While shopping in the doggy supermarket, grab a toy
    and try to run with it.

    Your human:

    a) Takes the toy away from you
      and puts it back.   0 points

    b) Takes the toy from you and
      puts it in the shopping basket.   1 point

    c) Lets you go to checkout
      with the toy.   2 points

    d) Grabs another toy in his teeth
      and runs out of the store with you.   3 points

6. While you're on leash, run around your human
    until her legs are all tied up.

    Your human:

    a) Untangles the leash with her hands.   0 points

    b) Stands still and whimpers.   1 point

    c) Rolls on the ground and howls.   2 points

    d) Bites through the leash to get free.   3 points

7. Hide a piece of cat poop under the couch.

    Your human:

    a) Never notices it.   0 points

    b) Keeps sniffing but doesn't locate it.   1 point

    c) Finds it and throws it out.   2 points

    d) Finds it and eats it.   3 points

8. Grab your human's most expensive piece of jewelry and put it out in the yard.

    Your human:

    a) Cries. 0 points

    b) Runs around in a circle, all excited. 1 point

    c) Fetches the jewelry and
    runs away with it. 2 points

    d) Fetches the jewelry and brings
    it back to you. 3 points

9. How many hours a day does your human sleep?

    a) 1 – 4 0 points

    b) 5 – 9 1 point

    c) 10 – 15 2 points

    d) 16 – 24 3 points

10. What does your human do immediately after bathing?

    a) Walks around soaking wet. 0 points

    b) Uses a towel to dry off. 1 point

    c) Shakes all the water off. 2 points

    d) Goes outside and rolls in the dirt. 3 points

11. What does your human do when you lick his face?

    a) Jerks his head away. 0 points

    b) Closes his eyes and makes a face. 1 point

    c) Looks at you and smiles. 2 points

    d) Licks you back. 3 points

12. How many toys does your human own that have names?

    a) 0 – 5 0 points

    b) 6 – 10 1 point

    c) 11 – 20 2 points

    d) More than 20 3 points

13. What does your human do while a passenger in a car?
   a) Sits quietly in the passenger seat.   0 points
   b) Goes to sleep on the floorboard.   1 point
   c) Sticks her head out of the window. 2 points
   d) Jumps on the driver's lap
      and helps steer.   3 points

14. What does your human do when frustrated?
   a) Lies down and sulks.   0 points
   b) Screams.   1 point
   c) Chews on the drapes.   2 points
   d) Gets the zooms.   3 points

15. What does your human do when in a crowd?
   a) Tries to hide.   0 points
   b) Stands in one place and trembles.   1 point
   c) Runs around and makes friends.   2 points
   d) Sniffs everyone's butt.   3 points

How does your human rate?

31-45 Points

You are a lucky dog! Your human has scored in the top rank. In fact, the results show an almost dog-like intelligence. You both often feel that you can read each other's mind. Humans who score this high are easily trained and usually make good work-humans. They thrive in new situations, are not easily frightened, and are good with puppies. Most humans in this category are female.

Along with such high intelligence, however, can come potential problems. Often such humans have dominant personalities and may even challenge your authority around the house. You may find yourself in a constant battle to maintain your leadership of the pack, with your human testing the limits at every opportunity.

You must remain consistent in your treatment of your human. If you are permissive even once, it can undo months of training. It's also good practice to regularly reassert your authority by, for example, making your human move away from her favorite spot on the couch so that you can lie there. Similarly, take away something she considers hers, such as the car key, and hide it. Give it back only when your human begins to cry and beg.

Another problem with highly intelligent humans is that, because they learn so quickly, they begin to anticipate your every move. If you want to go into the bedroom and steal a sock, they will close the bedroom door before you can get there. If you want to punish them for something they did by going poopy on the rug, they will see the signs and take you outside before you have a chance to complete your plan. But, with a little ingenuity on your part, you can use this trait against them in such a way that you can make them do whatever you want, whenever you want it.

Be firm but fair with your intelligent human, and she will make a happy and well-adjusted companion for as long as she lives.

16–30 Points

Your human has scored in the middle range. Although such humans will often exhibit dog-like acuity of mind, at other times they will revert to more human-like behavior, which is undesirable. Your goal in training is to reinforce the former and discourage the latter.

When your human does something right, such as sharing a snack, offer a reward of licks and kisses. There is no stronger motivator for humans than the prospect of love and affection. When they fall short, sternly bark, "No!" and attempt the action again. Even after you've achieved the desired training results, you must continue to work with your human to reinforce the proper behaviors. Unlike humans in the highest intelligence group, humans in the middle rank are somewhat unpredictable in their long-term retention of commands.

Humans in this middle group make wonderful playmates and usually will not dispute your role as master of the household.

0-15 Points

You've got big trouble here, puppy. Humans in this lowest rank exhibit almost no dog-like traits, are marginally trainable, and have almost no concept of being a member of a pack. The vast majority of such humans were raised with absolutely no contact with dogs, though the presence of cats is a common thread in the upbringing of these unfortunate humans. If you trace back far enough in their pedigree, you will almost certainly find an ancestor with obvious genetic damage, such as a politician, IRS worker, or rap music fan.

For those of you who must live with such humans, you must, from the very start, abandon any hope of long-term training success. The most you can reasonably aim for is to teach them to be somewhat conscious of their surroundings, enough so that they can sense trouble before it smacks them in the forehead. Nevertheless, you will often be called upon to warn your humans of danger and to lead them to safety when their observational deficiencies lead them astray.

Most humans in this lowest category are male.